BMW
Z SERIES
THE COMPLETE STORY

Other titles in the Crowood AutoClassic Series

BMW
Z SERIES
THE COMPLETE STORY

MICK WALKER

The Crowood Press

First published in 2003 by
The Crowood Press Ltd
Ramsbury, Marlborough
Wiltshire SN8 2HR

www.crowood.com

British Library Cataloguing-in-Publication Data
A catalogue record for this book is available from the British Library.

ISBN 1 86126 424 0

Typeface used: Bembo.

Typeset and designed by
D & N Publishing
Lowesden Business Park, Lambourn Woodlands, Berkshire.

Printed and bound in Great Britain by Bookcraft, Midsomer Norton.

Contents

Introduction

Ever since the early 1960s I have admired BMW's high engineering standards. At first this interest was centred on the company's motorcycles, the R69S flat-twin in particular; later it came to embrace their cars.

Besides quality, BMW also means 'driving experience'. Drive a BMW car and you will soon realize that it has been designed as a complete vehicle, not just one that fulfils a small number of tasks brilliantly, but fails miserably on the rest. And so it is with BMW's Z Series: not only have they been built to provide a sporting experience, but they excel in many areas where conventional sports cars often fail, such as comfort, durability, attention to detail, design, sophistication and the like.

The author piloting his 1998 Z3 2.8 around Mallory Park race circuit, Leicestershire, August 2001.

By far the best-selling of the Z Series has been the Z3. Although not always loved by the press, it has still racked up impressive sales figures – and the reason for this is simple. The Z3 has a wide range of versions, appealing to many pockets – and not only can you have considerable fun driving one, but all Z3s retain the attributes that make cars such as the 3 and 5 Series such a good buy, including an excellent residual value when the time comes to sell one on. There is also the advantage of BMW's comprehensive dealer network, something that many other makes of sports car marques simply cannot match, either in the number of dealers or the quality of service.

The Z Series began with the Z1 of the late 1980s. Conceived during the middle of that decade, it pre-dated the Japanese Mazda MX-5 by several years, and its German design team had the honour of creating the first modern compact roadster. But that said, the Z1 was too expensive to achieve what the Mazda went on to do; namely success in mass sales, due to an affordable purchase price. So it was left to the Z3 to get BMW's roadster ball off the ground – though of course BMW was not new to roadsters, far from it in fact, as the 328 of the 1930s and the 507 of the 1950s prove.

In compiling *BMW Z Series* I was fortunate in receiving help from many quarters. A big 'thank you' firstly to BMW, both at the British import arm in Bracknell and the Munich headquarters, and in particular to Chris Willows and Natalie Wakefield. Next comes the British dealer network, notably Sycamore's of Peterborough and to Brian Sleaford, Graham Stacy, Jez Wensor and Mark Flaxman-Binns. Thanks also to Ross Green of Dunedin BMW in Edinburgh, and Mark Griffin of the King's Lynn dealers, Sorensons.

Stuart Rowbottom provided considerable help with the 'M Roadster' chapter and illustrations. Several owners gave valuable assistance, including Roger Burt (Z1), Mrs Julie Winterman (Z3 1.9), Graham Clegg (Z3 2.0), Dave Williams (Z3 2.2), Peter Hemens (Z3 2.8), Brian Naylor (Z3 3.0), David Scott (M Roadster), Ian Davies (M Coupé) and Joseph Price (Z8).

Finally, thanks must go to Rita and Ian Welsh of Edinburgh who helped with much of the testing. During some three-and-a-half years I clocked up over 30,000 miles, testing a wide range of Z Series cars, ranging from a 1989 Z1 to a 2001 Z8, and to provide a comparison I also drove many rival manufacturers' cars, including the Lotus Elise, the Mazda MX-5, the MGF, the Porsche Boxster, the Mercedes SLK and the TVR Griffith.

I ended up appreciating the qualities of the Z3 to such an extent that I now own one myself – what else can I say!

Mick Walker
Wisbech, Cambridgeshire
March 2003

1   BMW Milestones

1916

Two engineers, Gustav Otto and Karl Rapp, founded Bayersiche Flugzeugwerk AG, located in the northern sector of Munich. With an initial stock capital of 200,000 Reichsmarks, the new company's exclusive production is aero engines.

1917

The company is renamed Bayersiche Motoren Werke (Bavarian Motor Works). The 500th aircraft engine leaves the plant.

1918

BMW is incorporated on the 13 August that year with the stock capital of 21 million Reichsmarks. Employees now total 3,500.

1919

Aircraft engine production comes to a halt due to the Treaty of Versailles, but testing is continued in secret. Franz Zeno Diemer sets up a new world altitude record of 9,760m (32,021ft) in a BMW-powered biplane. The Allied War Commission later confiscates all documents pertaining to the Diemer world record. BMW begins production of air brakes, agricultural machinery and metal castings for other companies.

On 9 June 1919 Franz Zeno Diemer set a new world altitude record of 9,760m (32,021ft) with a DFW biplane powered by a 250bhp six-cylinder BMW engine.

1920

BMW uses surplus aviation materials to manufacture tool cabinets and office furniture. A lightweight motorcycle with a single-cylinder two-stroke engine was marketed under the 'Flink' brand name.

1922

BMW begins series production of its first horizontally opposed motorcycle engine with transverse cylinders, for sale to other companies; it displaced 500cc and developed 6.5bhp.

1923

BMW's first brand-name motorcycle, the R32 494cc flat-twin with shaft final drive, is the star of the Paris show; it was the work of chief designer Max Friz.

1924

The company is now able to manufacture aero engines again, turnover is 8.3 million marks, and there are 1,200 employees.

1925

The motorcycle model range has increased to nine models, whilst BMW aero engines hold twenty-eight world records for speed, range, altitude and non-stop flights.

1927

The first BMW 750cc motorcycle, the R62, finishes testing and is ready for production. BMW builds its 25,000th motorcycle.

BMW's first series production motorcycle, the 494cc R32, was launched at the Paris Motor Show in 1923.

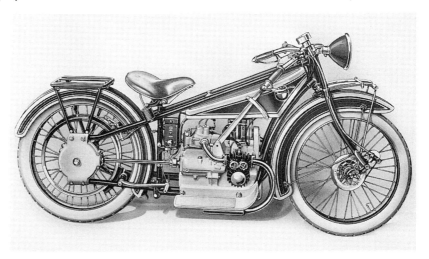

Between 1923 and 1926 a total of 3,100 R32 motorcycles were built at BMW's Munich works. With the acquisition of the Eisenach works in 1928, BMW was able to begin production of its first car, a licence-built British Austin Seven, sold under the Dixi label.

1928

BMW takes over the plant and licence agreement of the Eisenach works to manufacture the British Austin Seven. Sold in Germany as the Dixi, it was BMW's entry to the car world, whilst Eisenach was the centre of BMW car production until 1945. A total of 2,630 employees was on the payroll.

1929

Production of the Type 315/1 (Dixi) increases considerably, employee numbers are up to 3,860, and Ernst Henne riding a supercharged BMW twin, sets a new world motorcycle speed record.

The British Austin Seven, sold as the Dixi in Germany, is BMW's initial entry into the car world during the late 1920s.

Riding a supercharged BMW motorcycle, Ernst Henne smashes the world speed record in 1929. The bike is seen here at the Paris Motor Show that year.

1930

The Dixi wins the 750cc class at the Monte Carlo Rally. The gathering economic crisis, triggered by the American Wall Street stock-market crash of October 1929, begins to take effect.

1931

Whilst other German companies are going to the wall, BMW manages to continue without reducing its workforce, which now totals almost 4,000. More world records are gained, notably in the fields of aviation and railways.

1932

Ernst Henne sets a new world motorcycle speed record of over 152mph (244km/h). The first all BMW-designed car enters production, whilst the famous Junkers Ju52 aircraft enters service using three BMW air-cooled, nine-cylinder radial engines.

The famous Junkers Ju52 trimotor aircraft was powered by three 550hp nine-cylinder BMW 132 engines.

In 1931 a team of BMW 3/15s successfully completed a 10,000km (6,200 mile) endurance test around Berlin's Avus circuit without mechanical failures of any sort.

The nine-cylinder BMW 132 radial engine as installed in the Ju52.

1933

With its workforce now up to 4,720, BMW forges ahead in all its markets. This year also saw the arrival of the 303 car with its 1,175cc six-cylinder engine – a first of this engine type for the company.

1934

Record expansion at both the Munich and Eisenach plants sees the workforce reach 12,576.

1935

BMW produces the R12, the first series production motorcycle with telescopic front forks. The new German air force, the Luftwaffe, relies heavily on BMW engines, including the proven watercooled Mark IV and the new air-cooled 132 radial unit. A new aircraft engine plant is opened at Eisenach.

1936

BMW introduces a new two-litre, six-cylinder car with twin carburettors and 50bhp, known as the 326. The Reich Ministry of Aviation decides that in future BMW shall have exclusive production rights to manufacture air-cooled engines, whilst water-cooled engines shall be the responsibility of Daimler-Benz.

1937

The new 328 Roadster enters limited production. Although only ever sold in limited numbers, it goes on to achieve a legendary reputation in motoring circles for its all-round performance. Ernst Henne sets a new world motorcycle speed record of 279km/h (173mph), which was to remain unbroken for fourteen years. Almost 14,000 workers are now employed.

1938

The famous Mille Miglia in Italy was dominated by the BMW team with their 328 cars. They all finished the race, winning the team award. The German Alpine Tour and the Berlin Avus races were further victories. The 100,000th BMW motorcycle was built, and 18,624 people are on the payroll.

1939

In the year when World War II began, BMW's turnover jumps to 275 million Reichsmarks, and the company employs almost 27,000 workers. Georg 'Schorsch' Meier becomes the first foreigner to win the Senior TT on the Isle of Man, riding a supercharged BMW twin.

Georg 'Schorsch' Meier, riding a BMW, became the first foreign rider of a foreign bike to win the Isle of Man Senior TT, circa 1939.

1940

The legendary BMW 328 wins the Italian Mille Miglia, miles ahead of the competition. Production begins of an air-cooled twin radial aero engine with fourteen cylinders developing 1,800bhp.

1941

There are now 35,419 on the payroll, and a turnover of 385 million Reichsmarks. More performance is designed into the air-cooled twin radial aero engine: 2,200bhp. BMW engineers begin work on the 109-003 jet aero engine – the world's first production jet engine to power an aircraft.

1942

BMW has the largest staff in its history, 47,346 employees, with a turnover of 560.8 million marks.

1943

The 109-003 jet engine goes into series production.

1944

BMW engineers conceive an aircraft engine with a four-fold radial arrangement and twenty-eight cylinders, developing 3,600bhp and featuring twin counter-rotating airscrews. The Munich plant is destroyed by Allied bombing: reconstruction cannot take place until after the war.

1945

At the war's end, the largely destroyed Munich plant is confiscated; the Eisenach plant is now under Soviet rule.

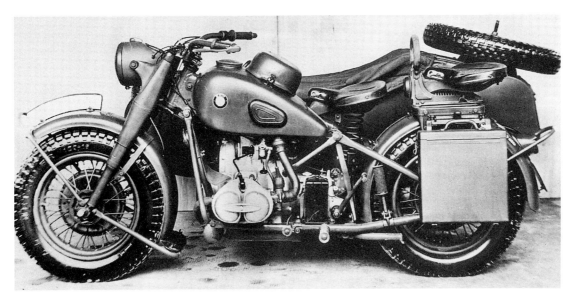

Probably the most famous German military vehicle of World War II: the BMW R75 motorcycle and sidecar. It served with distinction from the boiling heat of the African desert through to the Arctic wastes of a Russian winter.

1946

Tentative steps are taken at the Munich works. First products are manufactured from leftover scrap, including cooking pots, bakery utensils and agricultural machinery.

1948

A partial lifting of the ban on the production of vehicles allows BMW to resume motorcycle construction – though to start with, the R24 single-cylinder with 12bhp and shaft final drive is built, with a maximum engine size of 250cc.

1949

BMW produces and sells 9,450 motorcycles. New machine tools and plant arrive. The first post-war, twin-cylinder BMW motorcycle, the 500cc R51/2, is produced. The German mark regains its status as a hard currency.

1950

Motorcycle production increases to 17,100. Plans for resuming car production are already on the drawing board.

1951

25,000 motorcycles are built in this year. BMW car production begins again, with the six-cylinder 501 saloon coming off the Munich production line.

1953

Although BMW notches up its 100,000th motorcycle since the end of the war, a slump is coming in two-wheel sales as the general economy improves. The first German eight-cylinder car of the post-war period, the 502, makes its debut.

During the 1950s, BMW's car and motorcycle sales were not meeting targets, so in an attempt to improve matters it built the Isetta bubble car. Almost 200,000 of these tiny vehicles were sold, in what proved to be one of the company's few success stories of the decade.

1954/55

The motorcycle business continues to decline, even though BMW wins the world sidecar title. 'Hot' versions of the eight-cylinder car make their debut in the shape of the 503 cabriolet and 507 roadster. Both gain much praise and publicity, but few sales. The first Isetta bubble car comes off the line: it is a big commercial success and one which keeps the company afloat.

1956/58

Motorcycle sales prove to be on the slide, and sales of its big cars are low volume; only the tiny Isetta sells in any real quantity. Concern mounts as to the future of the Munich company.

1959

With the takeover of BMW by Daimler-Benz and Deutsche Bank only minutes away, a small group of shareholders headed by Dr Herbert Quandt saves the company.

1961

A new small BMW car, the 700, with an engine based on the 'boxer twin', proves to be a runaway success. The design and development offices begin work on a new series of cars.

1962

The first of the 'New Breed', the 1500 saloon, enters production and immediately becomes a top seller.

1964

An enlarged version, the 1600, arrives. Like the 1500, this is a compact, agile car with chassis, road-holding and driving performance second to none in its class.

Dr Herbert Quandt, the saviour of BMW in 1959 when the company was on the financial rocks. The Quandt family remain major BMW shareholders today.

In 1962 the 1500 saloon entered production. This was the first of the modern range of cars that can be traced to today's 3 Series. Later, but in the same decade, 1600, 1800 and 1800ti models were added.

From 1969, BMW's motorcycle production was transferred to a new factory at Spandau, Berlin.

1965

BMW produces 58,524 vehicles.

1966

A sports version, the 1600-2, makes its debut at the Geneva Motor Show. This is built as a two-seater coupé. BMW acquires Glas GmbH of Dingolfing.

1967

The 1600-2 coupé was followed by the 1600-2 cabriolet. This was a limited edition that BMW had commissioned with the help of specialists Baur, based in Stuttgart.

Between 1954 and 1974 BMW won no fewer than a record-breaking nineteen world motorcycle sidecar championship titles. The final six were won by Klaus Enders and Ralf Engelhardt (pictured).

The excellent E36 series of the 3 Series arrived in the early 1980, ranging from the 318 (90bhp) to the 323 (139bhp).

1968/70

The new 1800ti gains two victories in the international 24-hour race at Spa Franchor-champs in Belgium. In 1969, production climbs by a staggering 33 per cent to 145,000 cars. Motorcycle production is transferred to a new factory in Spandau, Berlin.

1971

BMW turns out 166,354 cars and 18,898 motorcycles. Inauguration of the new BMW test circuit, at the time the most advanced in the world. It allows not only high speed testing, but a handling course and crash test facilities.

1972

BMW's new headquarters opens in Munich. Known as the 'Four Cylinder Building' due to its shape, it forms a new landmark for the city.

The year 1978 saw the M1, BMW's first mid-engined sports car, make its debut; this became the first of the famous M (Motorsport) family.

In 1983 the Brazilian Nelson Piquet became the first 'turbocharged' world champion in Formula 1 racing, driving a 600bhp BMW-engined car.

1973

The turbocharger was relatively unexplored territory when BMW first applied the system to its 2002 model. The Bavarian manufacturer thus sparked a trend that was soon to be followed by Porsche, with its legendary 911 Turbo, the Saab, and eventually almost the entire car industry.

1978

The M1, BMW's first mid-engined sports car, makes its debut, thus becoming the first of the M (Motorsport) Series. Its 3,453cc, six-cylinder engine produced 277bhp, the racing version 470bhp.

1983

The Brazilian Nelson Piquet becomes the first 'turbocharged' world champion in Formula 1 racing, driving a Brabham BMW.

1987

BMW's first Z Series car arrives in the shape of the new Z1. It came thanks to a new 100-strong R&D wing, under the leadership of former Porsche engineer Ulrich Bez. Its design process, which incorporated several new ideas, took a mere two years from drawings to metal. Its 2,494cc in-line six produced 170bhp at 5,800rpm. The company became the first German car maker since the 1930s to introduce a twelve-cylinder power unit.

More M power, this time the 5.0litre, road-going V8 unit, circa the late 1980s.

1992

The 'breaking the ground' ceremony took place for the US plant at Spartanburg, South Carolina, on a new greenfield site. It was to be the production site for the company's forthcoming Z3 Series, and also marked a major step in BMW's globalization process.

1996

Making its world launch at the Detroit Motor Show, the Z3 was destined to become BMW's first massed-produced sports car; it was also the first car in the history of the company entirely built outside Germany.

1997

Six-cylinder versions of the Z3 make their debut in the shape of the 2.8 and, a few months later, the 3.2 M Roadster. The first right-hand-drive British Z3s (1.9) are finally delivered to 3,000-plus customers who have waited many

months. A Coupé version of the Z3M, causes controversy when launched in the autumn at the Frankfurt Show.

1998

Z3 2.8, Z3M Roadster and Z3M Coupé go on sale in the UK.

1999

At the Frankfurt International Motor Show, BMW presents the Z9 GT concept car. Equipped with a Common Rail direct-injection turbo-diesel engine, and carbon-fibre reinforced synthetic materials over an aluminium space-frame chassis, it offers key pointers to BMW's possible future direction.

2000

Available in left-hand drive, BMW launches its expensive, low volume, high performance sports car, the Z8. Powered by the 4,941cc V8 from the M5 saloon, the newcomer boasts 400bhp and is limited to 156mph (251km/h). Meanwhile, except for the Z3M Roadster and Coupé, the Z3 receives a mid-life face-lift.

2001

The sports version of the Z3, in 2.2 and 3.0-litre engine sizes, is launched. The X Coupé concept car is displayed. Its Chris Bangle-inspired styling will be followed by the Z4, the replacement for the Z3, launched at the Paris Show the following year.

2002

The Z4 arrives; its convex and concave styling, with sharp and rounded edges, creates a storm of controversy. Z3 ceases production after six years; almost 300,000 examples have been sold, making it BMW's best-selling roadster ever.

2   BMW – A Tradition with Roadsters

BMW's first car, known as the Dixi, received the official factory designation of 3/15; it was also built in roadster guise. It featured a removable hood and folding windscreen.

It is an interesting and little-known fact that BMW's very first car, the 1928 Dixi, coded 3/15 (based on the British Austin Seven), was also available as a roadster. Known as the Wartburg Sport, it was named after the castle that towered over the company's Eisenach plant, and was an open two-seater featuring a folding windscreen, low doors, and an 18bhp, 750cc, four-cylinder engine. And the 'Sport'

label was not misplaced, as was subsequently proved by its performance in rallies and circuit races, including a team victory in the 1929 Alpine Rally.

With the introduction in 1934 of the more sophisticated six cylinder 1.5 and 1.9 litre 315/1 and 319/1 models, BMW built on its original Roadster name. These cars featured classically shaped lines, with flowing integral wings, rear-wheel spats, and the now time-

In 1929 a three-car team of 3/15 Roadsters scored an impressive victory in the Alpine Rally.

honoured long bonnet and short tail. The 319 and 319/1 were not simply open versions of existing models, but genuine roadsters that made their mark in the world of racing – indeed, so much so, that in Great Britain the Aldington brothers, proprietors of the Frazer Nash concern, immediately applied to become the German company's official importers after being soundly beaten in the 1934 Alpine Rally. Almost 350 examples of these two models were built.

Enter the 328

The 319/1 led directly to the most famous of all pre-war BMW cars, the legendary 328, a car much sought after today as the benchmark two-litre sportster of its era. Producing 80bhp in standard form, and considerably more in

In production from 1937 until 1940, the superb 328 was considered by many as the best roadster of its time. A total of 464 cars were built.

The 328 Legend

The prototype 328 made its racing debut in 1936 during the annual Eifel race at the notorious 14-mile (22.5km) Nürburgring circuit. Driven by Grand Prix driver and world motorcycle speed record holder Ernst Henne – ironically under contract with rival Mercedes-Benz – it caused a sensation, winning first time out. And not only did it win, but the victory came in convincing fashion, with Henne immediately stamping his authority on the race, eventually winning by a huge margin over the second-placed competitor, a supercharged Alfa Romeo.

The following year, in 1937, the 328 Roadster entered limited production. Lightweight engineering and a perfectly balanced rear-wheel drive made this 1,971cc (66 × 96mm) six-cylinder inline-engined car ideal not only for fast road use, but also for motorsport. With just about enough room for two adults, the 328 weighed only 1,830lb (830kg), with its 80bhp being capable of pushing the BMW sportster along at a then very respectable 93mph (150km/h).

With its low weight and incredibly direct rack-and-pinion steering, the 328 could really show its pace on tight, twisting roads. At the front the suspension was taken care of by independently suspended wishbones and leaf springs, whilst at the rear the 328 had a rigid live axle and longitudinal leaf springs.

Unlike today's cars, the 328's priority was driving prowess, rather than features such as comfort, safety and environmental considerations. It was, in fact, a very basic car, but still a brilliantly conceived one. As one journalist put it: 'the two-litre, six-cylinder, inline beauty was fitted into a car stripped down to the bare essentials to produce a wonderful driving machine.'

At a time when the British dominated the roadster scene, the 328 made its debut in England and caused a real stir when it won the Tourist Trophy. This was followed by victory at the legendary Brooklands circuit near Weybridge in Surrey, and the list of wins was to grow over the next few years, culminating in a decisive victory in the gruelling 1,000-mile Mille Miglia in 1940, when Count Huschuke von Hanstein and co-driver Walter Bäumer took a tuned 328 to the chequered flag, setting a new course record of 103mph (166km/h).

Before this, in 1938, a standard 328 Roadster had scored a great victory in the famous Spa Franchorchamps 24-hour endurance race in Belgium; it had also scored its first Mille Miglia success.

continued overleaf

The 328 Legend *continued*

The 328 (1937)

Engine	Inline, six-cylinder, twelve-valve sohc, aluminium head, cast-iron block, liquid cooled
Displacement	1,971cc
Bore	66mm
Stroke	96mm
Transmission	Four-speed ZF or Hurth manual gearbox
Fuel system	Three × Solex downdraught 30JF carburettors
Doors	Two
Seats	Two
Chassis	Tubular steel main-members, with box-section cross-members
Bodywork	Part steel, part aluminium
Drive	Rear wheel
Wheels	16in front and rear
Tyres	5.25 × 16 front and rear ★

Dimensions

Overall length	3,900mm (153.5in)
Overall width	1,550mm (61in)
Overall height	1,400mm (55.1in)
Wheelbase	2,400mm (94.5in)
Dry weight	830kg (1,828lb)
Max power	80bhp @ 5,000rpm
Max torque	n/a
Top speed	93mph (130km/h)
0–62mph	10sec

★ Some cars delivered with wider rims and 3.50 × 16 tyres

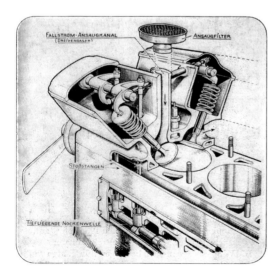

Technical drawing showing the cylinder head and block details of the 80bhp 328 engine.

racing guise, the 328 took the sporting world by storm, winning its class in virtually every race in which it competed between 1936 and 1940, and in the process humbling many larger displacement sports cars. The roll call of honour includes victories in such classics as Le Mans, the Mille Miglia, the Tourist Trophy, and countless other well known events, and was capped by overall victory in the final pre-war Mille Miglia. Only 464 examples of the magnificent 328 were built, but even so, it reaffirmed the Roadster, a tradition that has played such an important part in BMW's history.

The 328, in racing guise, dominated Europe's circuits in the years prior to World War II. In tuned form the six-cylinder engine could turn out 135bhp and reach speeds of 130mph (219km/h).

A works 328 taking part in the Austrian Alpine Rally, circa 1938.

One of the factory-supported 328s at the start of the Italian Mille Miglia in 1940.

The Roadster Revived

This tradition of BMW roadsters was revived in 1955 with two models, the 503 (a long-wheelbase, 140bhp, V8-engined cabriolet) and the highly acclaimed 507 sportster. The latter model, with its aluminium body, was a particularly sleek and seductive design, styled by Count Albrecht Goertz and capable of speeds up to 137mph (220km/h), depending upon the reduction ratio of the rear axle. The 3,186cc in-line V8 produced 150bhp.

However, beautiful as the 507 was, it was extremely costly to produce, and was a financial disaster for BMW. Only 252 examples of the 507 were actually built before production was halted.

The 507 – A True Classic

Back in 1955 Max Hoffman, at that time the largest import auto dealer in the USA, joined forces with BMW sales director Hans Grewenig to introduce a series of models for the burgeoning American market.

Convinced that export sales would prove a success with the right cars, Hoffman and Grewenig forged a transAtlantic alliance to build a car, as Hoffman described it: 'combining sporting performance with luxury, comfort and stylish appearance!' And it was Hoffman who commissioned Belgian industrial designer Count Albrecht Goertz to develop his ideas for what was eventually to become the legendary 507 Roadster.

Goertz, a student of the world-renowned designer Raymond Loewy (famous for several American design icons, such as the Coca-Cola bottle), was not an established car designer, more someone who played around with cars in his spare time (although after the 507 he was to pen the 1970s' Datsun (Nissan) 240 Z sports car). From Goertz's drawings, a new two-seater roadster, based on the earlier BMW 502, was designed and built. Also, and little remembered today, is the fact that Goertz was also responsible for the design of the BMW 503.

Both the 507 and the 503 (the latter in both coupé and cabriolet versions) were unveiled to the public late in 1955 at the International Frankfurt Motor Show.

The first 503 cabriolets were delivered in May 1956. The 507 didn't arrive in the showrooms until November 1956, the difference being that when it had appeared at Frankfurt a year earlier, BMW had yet to approve factory production of the 507.

The 503 and 507 shared the same basic 3,186cc (82 × 75mm) in-line, eight-cylinder engine, but whereas the 503 put out 140bhp, the 507's unit produced an extra 10bhp. The American version, running on a higher compression 9:1 ratio, was even more powerful, with 195bhp on tap.

The original 507 prototype was numbered 70001. The second pre-production car (70002) was displayed at Frankfurt, and at a number of other venues, including Paris, Geneva and at the Waldorf-Astoria Hotel in New York.

Between November 1957 and when production ceased in 1959, only 252 (including the pre-production prototypes 70001 and 70002) were built. This was for a number of reasons, none reflecting on the actual ability of the car, but rather an extremely high purchase cost, the state of the world economy at that time, and, most of all, BMW's own financial crisis, which came to a head during the late 1950s.

It is interesting to recall that the 507 attracted the likes of world motorcycling (and later car) champion John Surtees and Elvis Presley as paying customers. Add to that Georg Meier, the famous record breaker and racing car (Auto Union) and motorcycle (BMW) driver/rider who purchased the second pre-production prototype 70002 car and carried out a complete overhaul in his Munich BMW dealership, including fitting disc brakes.

But as regards Max Hoffman's dream of the 507 becoming a sales success in the US market, this was not to be – even with Elvis Presley buying his 507 during his army tour in Germany.

Nonetheless, today a well-looked-after 507 commands top billing at any classic car event, and if one comes up for sale, would fetch top money – as witnessed by the sale of the second prototype at Christies, Pebble Beach, California auction in August 2001, where the pre-sale estimate was between US$400,000–450,000.

Designed by the Belgian Count Albrecht Goertz, the 507 was a true classic of the 1950s. This is Goertz's original sketch of the car in early 1955.

The 507 – A True Classic *continued*

The 507 (1956)

Engine	V8, 16-valve, sohc, liquid cooled aluminium head and block
Displacement	3,186cc
Bore	82mm
Stroke	75mm
Transmission	Four-speed ZF manual gearbox, floor change
Doors	Two
Seats	Two
Chassis	Steel tube
Bodywork	Galvanized steel
Drive	Rear wheel
Wheels	16in front and rear
Tyres	6.00 H-16 front and rear

Dimensions

Overall length	4,838mm (172.4in)
Overall width	1,650mm (65in)
Overall height	1,300mm (51.2in)
Wheelbase	2,480mm (97.6in)
Dry weight	1,330kg (2,930lb)
Max power	Europe 150bhp @ 5,000rpm. USA 195bhp @ 5,200rpm
Max torque	Europe 235Nm @ 4,000rpm. USA n/a
Top speed	118–137mph (190–221km/h), depending on rear axle reduction ratio
0–62mph	Europe 11.1 seconds. USA 8.7 seconds

The 507 – Annual Production Figures

1955	2
1956	1
1957	103
1958	99
1959	47
Total	252

Chassis numbers from 70001 to 70254
Note: There were two chassis-only deliveries.

An illustration of the 507 (with hardtop) from the original factory brochure. The car could reach speeds up to 137mph (221km/h), depending on specification.

Between November 1957 and when production ceased in 1959, only 252 examples of the 507 were constructed. This was due to various factors, including the high price, the depressed state of the car market, and BMW's own perilous financial position.

A New Approach

BMW hit the financial rocks in 1959, and only escaped takeover at the eleventh hour. This led the company to focus on developing core products that could guarantee a financial return, and some three decades were to pass before its next genuine two-seater roadster appeared in the shape of the late 1980s Z1. This was the brain-

child of the newly formed think-tank, BMW Technik GmbH. Investigating innovative technology led this team to examine lightweight engineering, new chassis concepts, door design and a new rear axle layout.

The resulting car featured a steel and composite-fibre chassis, removable and recyclable plastic body panels, the Z-axle that subsequently became part of the 3 Series, and, perhaps

A 507 shown with hardtop fitted. It is interesting to recall that the 507 attracted the likes of world car and motorcycling champion John Surtees and pop star Elvis Presley as owners.

The only man to have been world champion on two and four wheels, John Surtees (left) with the 507 he has owned since new in the late 1950s.

most famously, drop-down electric doors. Using the 170bhp 325i six-cylinder engine, the Z1 drove, as one journalist put it, 'like a go-kart', and even with a high purchase price found some 8,000 buyers in its three-year production run from 1988 through to 1991.

Then came a five-year break before customers were able to think about buying and owning another BMW roadster – and when they did, it was to be very much more accessible than anything the German company had been able to offer before the Z3, and the start of a global success story.

3 The Z1 – The First of the Series

The first of the Z Series, the Z1 project began in the mid-1980s, with the first prototype arriving in 1986; it went on sale in 1988.

During the 1980s BMW had gone some way to shedding its rather upper-crust but boring reputation with the introduction of performance saloons such as the M3 and M5. However, it was the Z Series that did most to change the perception of the Munich company's products, and it was probably the first of these, the Z1, which helped the most.

BMW Technik

One of the driving forces behind the formation of the 100-strong BMW Technik was Dr Wolfgang Reitzle: he realized that an élite corps of engineers was needed whose purpose was to find answers that the 6,000-strong development department could not. The first task, begun in 1985, was a brief 'to produce something that would show BMW to be on

Dpl. Ing. Wolfgang Reitzle

Dpl. Ing. Wolfgang Reitzle was the driving force behind many of the Z Series cars. He was head of BMW Technik between its establishment in 1985 and his leaving BMW in 1999 as the result of a boardroom reshuffle.

Wolfgang Reitzle was born on the 7 March 1949 in the Neu-Ulm district of Bavaria. From 1955 until 1967 he attended first an elementary school, and later a grammar school in Ulm; at the latter he took his final exams during 1967. Later in 1967 he began studying mechanical engineering at Munich Technical University, where he graduated as an engineer (*Diplom-Ingenieur*) in 1971.

At the beginning of 1972 he became scientific assistant at the Institute of Materials and Processing Science at Munich Technical University. Then in July 1974 he gained his doctor's thesis in engineering.

Also during the 1972–1975 period Reitzle studied labour and economic science at Munich Technical University, graduating as DWI (*Diplom Wirtschafts Ingenieur*).

In January 1976, Dpl. Ing. Wolfgang Reitzle joined BMW in Munich as a specialist in production technology; in April that year he was promoted to become boss of the Methods Testing Department. A year later, in April 1977, he was made head of the Process Engineering General Department.

By now Reitzle had not only become established in BMW's management structure, but was displaying his considerable engineering skills. More promotions followed: in February 1978 he was put in charge of the Pilot Plant and Process Engineering Division; in November 1981 he was made head of Engine Production, Parts Production and of the Foundry Division. In these latest roles his title of 'division manager' gave him the right to sign on the company's behalf for the first time.

From May to December 1983 he became assistant to the chairman of the board in the management of the R&D division of BMW. During the period January through to April 1984 Dpl. Ing. Reitzle attended the AMP (Advanced Management Programme) of the American Harvard Business School in Boston.

On his return to Germany, Reitzle became head of the Technical Central Planning Division of BMW, Munich. And because of his experience with research and development, he played a key role in establishing BMW Technik when it was formed in the spring of 1985. From July 1987 Reitzle's increasingly important role in the company had been recognized by his appointment as a full member of the Board of Management of BMW AG, and he was put in charge of R&D. Because of his power and foresight, Reitzle was able to ensure that BMW Technik remained outside the mainstream of the company's engineering so he could work on new concepts.

But then came the takeover of the British Rover Group, and together with Bernd Pischetsrieder, Reitzle was appointed to the Rover board whilst retaining his existing functions with the parent company back in Germany. His task at Rover was to develop a new range of models with which to replace the existing Honda-inspired cars that Rover had built during its sixteen-year relationship with the Japanese company.

As history records, the Rover–BMW marriage was a costly failure and Reitzle, together with Pischetsrieder, was forced to resign in a boardroom battle during early 1999. He later joined the Ford Motor Company, only to leave them in the spring of 2002. However, Wolfgang Reitzle's legacy at BMW is truly massive, not only in general engineering terms, but there is little doubt that without his foresight and leadership, none of the Z Series cars would have been built. And his final exit signalled the end of the era both for himself and BMW.

the right track again, blending innovation with a sense of fun, and yet retaining all the important qualities of safety and sound engineering'. The answer was to build a roadster – and remember that at the time the breed was at an all-time low, and Mazda's industry-changing MX5 was not yet on the horizon.

After a mere three months the first scale model was completed, and within six months a full-size clay mock-up was ready for presentation to the board of directors. Exactly twelve months after the decision was taken to build a prototype, one was ready to be test-driven – a perfect first birthday presentation

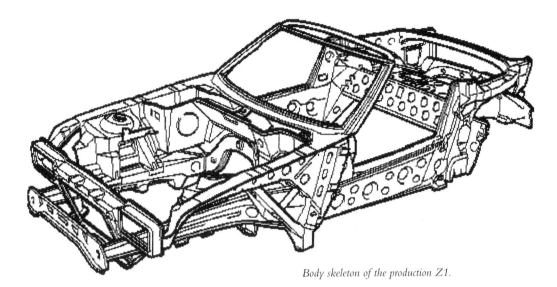

Body skeleton of the production Z1.

for the new department. The latter was now headed by former Porsche engineer Ulrich Bez, who was to work at BMW from 1982 to 1988, and later designed a whole range of models for the Korean marque Daewoo in the 1990s.

Many feel that the Z1 is the finest of the Z Series. From a sports car viewpoint, its handling and road-holding abilities cry out for more than the 170bhp 325i six-cylinder engine is capable of.

By the completion of the first prototype in 1986, the new roadster had been coded Z1. Why Z1, you may ask? Well, at the start the official definition was actually ZE1, which stood for *Zentral Engwicklung 1*, meaning 'Central Development number 1'.

The Design Evolves

The most striking design features of the Z1 project were its combination of existing BMW component parts, and future thinking in regard to advanced technology.

Although Dipl. Ing. Bez was in overall charge, BMW Technik hired Harm Lagaay from Ford of Europe as its design chief for the Z1 project. Lagaay recently explained:

I got to Munich in May 1985, three months after the group was set up. The type of car was settled, but the big question was whether it should be front-, mid- or rear-engined. I didn't hesitate in backing the engineers' leaning towards a front-mounted engine. If we'd gone for a rear engine, they'd have had all the problems of developing a new drive-train package, cracking the problems of driver position, weight distribution, crash protection, noise insulation and luggage space.

Mechanically, it was decided to make use of the powertrain and front suspension of the company's then current E30 325i, together with a new steel monocoque chassis and bolt-on plastic panels for the body. For good measure, there was also a brand-new form of rear suspension.

The Z1 (1989)	
Engine	Liquid-cooled, inline, six-cylinder, twelve-valve sohc, alloy head, cast-iron block
Displacement	2,494cc
Bore	84mm
Stroke	75mm
Transmission	Five-speed, manual
Fuel system	Multi-point fuel injection
Doors	Two
Seats	Two
Chassis	Steel, monocoque; zinc-plated
Bodywork	Plastic
Drive	Rear wheel
Wheels	16in front and rear
Tyres	Front 225/45 ZR16
	Rear 225/45 ZR16
Dimensions	
Overall length	3,921mm (154in)
Overall width	1,690mm (66.5in)
Overall height	1,277mm (50.2in)
Wheelbase	2,447mm (96.3in)
Dry weight	1,250kg (2,750lb)
Max power	170bhp @ 5,800rpm
Max torque	164lb ft (222Nm) @ 4,300rpm
Top speed	136mph (219km/h)
0–62mph	7.9 seconds

A Monocoque Chassis

At 1,250kg (2,750lb), the completed Z1 couldn't be called a lightweight, but it was very strong. Its backbone was a welded and fully zinc-cooled, steel monocoque chassis that carried all the mechanical parts, and to which the composite-fibre sandwich floor-plan and plastic panels were fitted. The high side sills of the monocoque achieved two things: they provided full side-impact protection, whilst also allowing the doors and windows to slide down out of sight for what BMW called 'the full open air feeling'. The system also gave, for the time, unprecedented side protection.

The Suspension System

The front suspension was the single-joint spring MacPherson system from the E30 3 Series, but with the track increased by 50mm (2in) and with increased caster to provide superior

---

The Z1: Technical Innovations

The Z1 was a significant car, not only because it was the first of BMW's Z Series, but also because of its pioneering construction, aerodynamics and new rear suspension system.

Chassis

The all-steel monocoque chassis was galvanized, and the zinc that filled in between the welds increased its torsional stiffness by an amazing 25 per cent. Rigidity was further helped by the deep side sills, the rear cross-panel, the strong tube integrated within and connecting the windscreen pillars, whilst the transverse tube ran behind the facia.

The innovative – unique in fact – composite-fibre sandwich underfloor added an additional 10 per cent to the monocoque's torsional rigidity. It was developed to be corrosion and crash resistant, to have the capacity to carry heavy loads, whilst at the same time provide a smooth, aerodynamic underpan; and it had the amazingly low weight of 15kg (33lb).

The Z1's monocoque chassis was exceedingly strong. Its backbone was a welded and fully zinc-coated steel assembly that carried all the mechanical parts, and to which the composite-fibre sandwich floor pan and plastic body panels were affixed. The original prototype structure is shown here.

Body Skin Panel Work

The plastic body panels had no load-bearing role in the Z1's structure; they could be removed or replaced within half an hour. The front and rear side panels were of Xenoy, a hi-tech thermoplastic that was virtually impact damage-free at speeds of 5mph (8km/h) or less.

The Z1 was the world's first production car to be built with all its vertical body parts manufactured from injection-cast thermoplastics. The development team, together with its suppliers, solved potential problems of panel rippling and paint finish and adhesion with an entirely new type of paint called Varioflex.

continued overleaf

The Z1: Technical Innovations *continued*

Door Design

The door design was another Z1 innovation. Sliding between the monocoque's sills and the outer dress panels, the doors and the windows with them were operated by electric motors and toothed belts. These latter components were housed in the car itself, rather than in the doors.

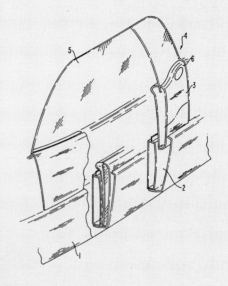

A feature of the Z1 was its patented door operation. The high sills of the monocoque chassis not only provided full side-impact protection, but allowed the doors to slide down out of sight (see pictures). BMW called this system 'the full open-air feeling'.

Factory drawing of the sliding door design. It was invented by Klaus Gersmann, working for BMW in Munich.

Rear Suspension

BMW named the Z1's innovative rear suspension 'Z-axle', and described it as a 'centrally guided, spherical, double wishbone system'. This new rear assembly embraced Porsche 928-like theories of controller camber and generating toe-in at high cornering forces. Up to 0.65g, it maintained slight toe-out, then induced toe-out. Apart from offering outstanding control of the wheel angles, and anti-squat and anti-dive, its design advantages were less weight and greater simplicity.

Aerodynamics

The BMW Technik design team fully appreciated the benefits of aerodynamics, and therefore put a considerable amount of work into achieving the most slippery shape possible on the Z1. Concave shaping of the bonnet between the wheel arches (possible because the engine was placed behind the axle line) did the work of a front wing. Another key factor was the full-length underfloor. The design team also mounted the silencer transversely under the tail: this was wing-shaped to work like an airfoil and cut lift.

The Z1 Annual Production Figures	
1986 & 1987	12
1988	58
1989	2,400
1990	4,091
1991	1,451
Total	8,012 (of which only 72 came to Great Britain)
Chassis numbers from AL00001 to AL08012	

directional stability and steering response, given the decrease of load on the front axle.

The rear suspension comprised a totally new system created by BMW Techniks Dipl. Ing. Rudolf Müller. Theoretically it could be compared to the Porsche Weissach axle and the Mercedes Benz multi-link system, but in practice it was much lighter and simpler, and was able to maintain its settings with a truly superb level of reliability and low maintenance.

The 325i Powerplant
The engine was lifted straight out of the E30 325i saloon: electronically managed, fuel-injected, single overhead cam, 2,494cc (84 × 75mm), two valves per cylinder, inline, six cylinder, it put out 170bhp at 5,800rpm, giving the Z1 a maximum speed of 136mph (219km/h) and a 0–62mph (0–100km/h) figure of 7.9sec.

This power was transmitted via the standard 3 Series five-speed gearbox through a rigid aluminium tube housing the tailshaft to the rear differential. This arrangement, in which the differential was connected by the tube to the gearbox, was in fact similar to the Porsche and Alfa Romeo transaxle systems, and gave the Z1 further stiffness.

Weight Distribution
BMW Technik's engineering team paid considerable attention to the Z1's weight distribution, finally achieving a 51 front/49 rear balance for the production vehicle. This was partly

achieved by the almost central engine location, it being some 300mm (11.8in) behind the front axle. A benefit of this location was that it enabled the engineering team, together with the aerodynamic specialists, to fully exploit the underbody for ground effects, knowledge gained from the company's Brabham F1 racing involvement.

Aerodynamics
Placing the engine so far back – almost 305mm (1ft) further back than in the 3 Series – and moulding the body in advanced plastics, allowed the design team enough flexibility to come up with aerodynamic solutions that provided slippery lines (a Cd factor of 0.36 with the hood up, and 0.43 with it down). In addition, it gave the correct kind of directional stability and zero lift, all without recourse to spoilers.

By placing the engine as far back as possible (almost 305mm (1ft) further back than in the 3 Series), and by moulding the body in advanced plastics, the Z1's development team were able to provide a Cd factor of 0.36 with the hood up, and 0.43 with it down.

The Z1's rear section was just as streamlined as the front. Part of the under-car airflow was directed over the silencer to exit from within the rear bodywork, just below the boot-lid.

Actually this is not quite true, as there were two spoilers on the Z1 – although a casual observer wouldn't notice either: the first was a concave section in the steeply raked centre section of the bonnet; the other, and probably unique to a production road car, was the rear silencer. Lying horizontally across the Z1's under-tail, this was shaped in a section akin to an airfoil. Some air flowed under this and onwards from under the car in a relatively conventional manner; another part of the under-car airflow was directed over it, to exit from within the rear bodywork just below the bootlid. This subtle approach was all part of a design harmony that made the Z1 significant for its lack of visible spoilers and the like, giving a general cleanliness to the overall appearance of the car.

The Z1 with roof erected. The hood was operated manually, not electrically, but unlike some it was easy to operate.

Front light cluster. It was designed to integrate into the bodywork and thus not hinder the search for good aerodynamics.

The Interior Design

When sitting at the wheel of the Z1, one is always given the feeling of being in something special. The cabin – leather throughout (or optional fabric/leather for the seating) – and the 370mm three-spoke steering wheel feel exactly right. The four round dials are the speedometer, tachometer and analogue display for fuel and coolant thermometer; the digital clock is in the central console, whilst the reinforced bucket seats are colour co-ordinated at the rear. The driver's seat is adjustable for height as well as reach, and this makes it really easy to get comfortable. Conventional period BMW ergonomics applied to the minor controls of the Z1, which meant the footwell was roomy and the pedals easy to operate.

The four instruments. The electronic speedometer is larger than the tachometer. The other two register fuel and coolant temperature.

Central console, with heater control, radio/cassette and clock. The lower area next to the gearlever includes a cigarette lighter, an ashtray and window switches.

Fuel filler cap.

Tool kit.

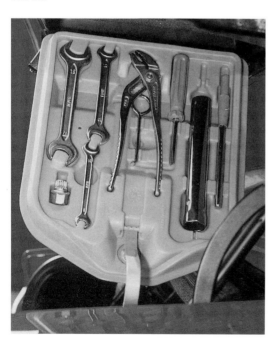

Rear light cluster.

Boot space is compromised by the spare wheel.

Refinement was excellent, and virtually up to BMW saloon levels, which made driving the Z1 the same silky affair as taking charge of a 325i. The power-assisted steering was light and fluid, as was the clutch and gear-change. Ride, too, was much better than one might have expected for a car that was, after all, billed as a sports roadster. A 1988 *Autocar* road test by Mel Nichols had this to say of the Z1's arrival:

> What the Z1 does is to bring luxury convertible refinement to the squat, compact, nimble Roadster

– and sets new standards for both. Its seats are outstandingly comfortable, its top is very easy to put up and down (it folds under the lift-up tonneau behind the cabin) and it is tight and snug and pretty quiet up to 100mph [160km/h]. The finish is superb, the boot is adequate for bags carrying two people's clothing for a few days away, and a removable cockpit dividing panel makes way for two pairs of skis.

However, only seventy-two Z1s were officially imported into Great Britain. A retail price of over £37,000 in 1990 didn't help – some

Hood and doors down, the Z1 can provide true open-air motoring and is unlike any other sports car in this respect, except specialist cars such as the Caterham and Westfield.

Left-hand drive only. Of the 8,000-plus built, only a mere seventy-two were officially imported into the UK.

£10,000 more than on the German home market. *Top Gear* presenter and TV personality Jeremy Clarkson admitted in March 1997 to paying £22,000 for a well-used example of a Z1 – for his wife. Not the world's biggest BMW fan; but Jeremy had to admit that he enjoyed driving the Z1 himself...

Probably the biggest question is, why didn't BMW develop the original Z1, instead of bringing out a brand new roadster a few years later? The answer is, of course, about economics – the Z1 was not a practical option. BMW needed a car that could be mass produced and make money; the result was the Z3.

Alpina Z1

Although Alpina has taken a luke-warm interest in the later Z Series cars, the Z1 was given the Bavarian tuning specialists full attention with their own version, the RLE (Roadster Limited Edition). Built in 1989, only sixty-six examples of the Alpina Z1 RLE were constructed, and today it is already becoming highly sought after by collectors.

At the heart of the RLE was the 2,693cc Alpina-developed engine, already in production for the C2 2.7 model, based on the E30 325i. Alpina were able to boast of a significant power increase over the standard Z1, up from 170bhp to a very healthy 204bhp.

With special pistons and camshaft, together with a revised and re-ported cylinder head and a reprogrammed engine management system, the 2.7 Z1 put out 195lb ft of torque (compared to the standard unit's 164lb ft figure).

Externally the Z1 RLE 2.7 was visually little changed from the stock car, except for a set of Alpina's trademark 17in alloy wheels and the company's Deco-Set gold side stripes. However, performance had certainly received an upgrade, 0–62mph (0–100km/h) being despatched in a mere 7.1sec, almost a second quicker than the normal Z1. Likewise maximum speed had increased from 136mph (219km/h) to 142mph (228km/h).

As for purchase price (no Alpina Z1 RLEs were officially sold in Great Britain), the 2.7 car cost DM116,000, as compared to the standard Z1 DM89,000. Which, if the Alpina Z1 had been marketed in Great Britain, would have meant a £50,000 price tag! This explains why it remained a German-market product.

The Griffin Z1 Conversion

Most would agree that the Z1's big weakness – and probably its only real one – was its lack of power. 170bhp may sound fine, but with a curb weight of 1,337kg (2,948lb), it was considerably heavier than it looked.

Enter the Griffin Motorsport Z1 conversion, that saw the engine displacement raised from 2,494cc to 2,693cc. This gave 224bhp (standard 170bhp) and 205lbft torque (standard 164lbft).

Lift the bonnet of the Griffin-converted Z1 and the engine *looked* standard, but underneath the engine casings it was a different story. Besides the bigger displacement, the modified engine employed a long-throw crankshaft from the long-defunct 525 era, lightweight Mahle 9.9:1 pistons and new connecting rods. A modified cylinder head with re-profiled porting and a hot camshaft (provided in Great Britain to Griffin's specification from one-off chill-cast blanks), reprogrammed Bosch Motronic engine management system, and an exhaust system designed for right-hand drive (part of the Griffin conversion) gave an additional 54bhp and much improved torque.

Griffin's RHD conversion was not easy, and represented a lot of engineering effort, as BMW never planned to make such a conversion and, as such, no RHD facia was available 'off the shelf'. Griffin Motorsport therefore had to produce its own dashboard. To achieve an accurate reversal, the original assembly was removed and a jig constructed to determine the attachment points. Once the leather and padding had been removed, it was sliced into five sections. These were then reassembled in the jig, *in situ* modifications were carried out, and a new mould was taken, from which the RHD-drive facia could be manufactured.

A bigger problem was the big bulge in the Z1's composite floorpan to accommodate the exhaust system, which on the Z1 ran to the right of the propshaft. This meant less space for the pedals and ensured a compromise was needed. It also entailed working with each customer of a Griffin Z1 conversion to ensure the most suitable pedal position.

With a standard Z1 costing £36,925 in Great Britain in 1990, the extra £11,706 for the Griffin conversion (engine modification plus RHD) sent the price soaring to £48,631.

When David Vivian tested the Griffin Motorsport Z1 for *Autocar* in 1990, he soon discovered that there was a somewhat compromised driving position, due to the RHD instead of the original LHD, and inferior brakes (again due to the transition from left to right). However, this was more than offset by gaining the power with which to exploit one of the great contemporary chassis. The Z1 'was always a suitable case for treatment and this is just what the doctor ordered, even if the price' Vivian commented 'was purely Harley Street'.

Griffin Motorsport Conversion Comparison

	BMW Z1	Griffin Z1		BMW Z1	Griffin Z1
Engine					
Displacement (cc)	2,494	2,693	*Fourth gear*		
Max bhp	170	224	30–50	8.8	7.3
Max torque (lb ft)	164	205	50–70	9.4	7.8
Overall mpg	24.0	23.0	70–90	9.6	7.2
Performance			*Fifth gear*		
Max speed (mph)	136	139	50–70	13.2	10.2
0–60	7.9	7.0	70–90	n/a	13.2
0–100	23.3	18.9			
Standing ¼ mile	15.9	15.4	Price	£36,925	£48,631
Third gear					
20–40	6.1	5.1			
40–60	5.7	4.8			
60–80	5.9	4.7			

Internal and external dimensions

Four-view drawing of the production Z1 from the 1989 factory brochure. Measurements given are in millimetres.

4 America, not Europe

BMW's management in both the 1950s and 1980s learned a hard lesson: you can't make money out of a high-priced, limited-volume roadster. However highly acclaimed and good the respective 507 and Z1 were, they both suffered the same fate. And not only this, but the arrival of Mazda's best-selling MX-5 had proved that there was money to be made *if* the approach was right. So for its new, high-volume 1990s roadster, BMW decided to make sure it offered a car that would both sell in large numbers on a worldwide basis, and make money at the same time.

As explained in Chapter 5, the new roadster, coded Z3, made considerable use of existing BMW technology and component parts, notably the 3 Compact Series. This was one way of attacking the costs issue. Another was the cost of building the car, which in Germany would have been the same as other 'Made in Germany' vehicles – high. Another was shipping costs to the perceived biggest market for the new roadster, the USA.

BMW Turns to America

By 1990, when the initial planning of the new car was first mooted (the same year the Mazda MX-5 Roadster went on sale), BMW was already well on the way to establishing a global network not only of sales organizations, but also of assembly and production facilities. Besides its plants in Germany at Munich, Dingolfing, Spandau (motorcycles) and Regensburg, there were also facilities at the Austrian

Steyr engine plant, and near Johannesburg, South Africa. In addition BMW had assembly plants in Mexico, Thailand, Vietnam, the Philippines, and other Pacific Rim countries.

So the company's board of directors back at the BMW headquarters building in Munich had no reason for building the Z3 in Germany. Quality was obviously a vital issue – no good saving money if warranty claims would shoot up. Although some European countries would have been cheaper on labour costs (Spain, for example), the shipping costs to the USA would have remained the same. So why not consider building the car in the USA?

Also, by 1990 the USA had become BMW's largest market outside Germany – and the US government had a positive climate towards business, and right from the start was very keen to attract BMW to the continent as a manufacturer.

South Carolina is Selected

By 1991 South Carolina had been selected, the reasons being the availability of a ready-made workforce, competitive rates of pay as compared to other states, and a willingness by the local authorities to assist with training and the selection process (an amazing 80,000 personnel ultimately applied to join the new manufacturing plant, for fewer than 2,000 positions).

Another key factor was the presence of excellent transportation systems: a deep-water port at Charleston, a major airport, and a modern rail and road network offering easy reach to BMW's primary markets. Also, critically important was the willingness of a wide range of component suppliers to establish production facilities nearby.

Building up to Production Status

The gestation period for the study, selection, announcement and building of the new plant at Spartanburg near Greenville, South Carolina, was done in almost record time for an auto maker setting up manufacturing facilities in a new country for the first time. From the ground-breaking ceremony on 30 September 1992 it was to take less than two years before the first production car, a 318i saloon, left the line. By March 1995 production of customer 318s was under way, prior to the presentation of the first Z3 Roadster in the autumn of 1995.

Production Begins

Full-scale production of Z3 1.9 models (the first Z3s) began in March 1996, and by the end of that year, 35,500 Z3 Roadsters had been delivered to customers. To cope with the worldwide demand for the new car, 318i production ceased during the same year, proving if nothing else the flexibility of BMW's new manufacturing plant to respond in changes to market needs.

Production of RHD (right-hand drive) Z3s started in December 1996 (mainly for Japan and Great Britain), whilst in the same month a second model, the Z3 2.8, started being built for the US domestic market. Left-hand-drive European cars followed in March 1997, with right-hand drive beginning by that summer. Finally the Z3 M Roadster and Coupé arrived a few months later still.

The Spartanburg facilities, near Greenville, South Carolina were constructed in near record time for an auto manufacturer setting up a manufacturing plant in a new country for the first time.

BELOW: *Full-scale production of the first Z3 models (1.9 four-cylinder) began at Spartanburg in March 1996, and by the end of that year a total of 35,500 Z3s had been delivered.*

The Spartanburg Plant

By the time Z3 production began, the Spartanburg plant occupied 1.2 million square feet on a 1,039-acre (420ha) site, which had plenty of room for additional expansion. There were some 1,900 employees who worked in a state-of-the-art manufacturing facility featuring systems that were environmentally as friendly as any auto manufacture can be regarding waste water treatment, emissions, and recycling programmes to reduce landfill waste, and a water-based paint shop. Proof of just how efficient BMW's Spartanburg manufacturing plant was at that time, is that it received an ISO 9002 certificate – an international quality standard for the industry. It was one of only two US automobile manufacturing plants to achieve this standard.

By February 1997, total investment of the Spartanburg facilities had risen to $800 million, with the daily output of Z3s being 255 cars. At that time, management declared the daily

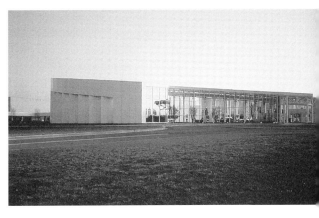

The Spartanburg plant was a state-of-the-art construction project carried out on a green-field site.

Part of the Spartanburg production line, with Z3 1.9s under construction.

production potential to be 300 units with the existing plant; however, an extension currently under construction would provide a future maximum output of 400 cars per day (90,000 per annum). Local content of the Z3 was 55 per cent by value, and rising. Engine and drive trains were shipped from Europe, whilst there were sixty-five North American component suppliers.

Thanks to the 318i saloon production, Spartanburg was not an entirely new facility when it began Z3 production. This fact, together with European-built major mechanical components such as engines, gearboxes, clutches and drive assemblies, meant that there were few real problems with the early cars – and no greater than any other start-up model could have expected to provide. In addition, BMW sent a team of Munich-based technicians and assembly workers to Spartanburg to assist the launch process.

ABOVE LEFT: As this photograph shows, Coupés and Roadsters are built together on the same production line; likewise the standard Z3 and M Series cars.

ABOVE: A 2.8 Coupé (not sold in the UK) being given its final inspection on the Spartanburg line, circa 1998.

An M Coupé in the Spartanburg factory.

5 The Z3 Arrives

When creating their Z3 Roadster (officially coded E36/7), BMW wanted to create a distinctive and affordable sporting product. The father of the Z3 project was Dipl. Ing. Burkhard Goeschel. Originally a motorcycle designer, Dr Goeschel has not only led the development team for the Z3, but has also been responsible for the development of the Z8 Roadster and the X5. It is also interesting to note that the Z3 project first began towards the end of the 1990s, when production of the Z1 had only just begun and the Mazda MX-5's success was not apparent.

A vital component in making the Z3 Series a success was not to fall into the trap of high production costs, the Z1's Achilles heel. So Dr Goeschel and his engineering squad looked to existing BMW component parts to, in the main, create the new car. In practice, this meant the Z3 being based around somewhat old technology, with elements of the new car (the rear suspension layout) dating back to the pre-1990 E30 3 Series and the Compact. Even so, there was much to applaud. But with its long nose and short tail, its reception was decidedly mixed. When it was launched, the first models to go on sale were the 115bhp 1.8 and the 140bhp 1.9, both with four-cylinder powerplants.

This in turn led to a mixed press reception. Maybe if BMW had launched the six-cylinder 2.8 or the stunning M version, much of the criticism wouldn't have been levelled at the newcomer in the way it was.

Road-Testing the Z3 1.9 (1996)

The 140bhp, four-cylinder, sixteen-valve, 1.9-litre version of BMW's new roadster was the first Z3 to go on sale (in left-hand-drive form), together with the smaller eight-valve 1.8 model in early 1996. Only the 1.9 came to the UK, however, and by the time it went on sale, BMW GB had over 3,300 outstanding orders (actually 3,306) by its official showroom launch; dealer demonstrators were delivered in February 1997, with the first customer model arriving the following month. The first customers, all of whom had paid deposits, had been waiting several months; they paid a shade under £20,000, with the UK price standing at £20,560 for new orders in the spring of 1997. But even though the press road-tests of the time usually bemoaned the 'lack of performance' and 'compact under-pinnings', the 1.9 *did* represent a good buy and offered a price considerably less than that from Mercedes or Porsche.

What you got was a great-looking car with rear-wheel drive, a superb gearchange (which is better than the larger sixes (the 2.8 and the 3.0 and the M Roadster), excellent brakes, and acceleration to match most GTI-type hatches – a 0–62mph (100km/h) figure of 9.5sec.

On the road, the 1.9 proves a game performer, featuring a rev-happy (and smooth) four-cylinder engine with its own exhaust rasp. But it never comes across as a truly rapid car. On the other hand, it has excellent levels of smoothness and refinement when cruising or using the motorway. Like the rest of the Z3 range, it's a comfortable way to travel.

continued overleaf

Road-Testing the Z3 1.9 (1996) *continued*

Wind buffeting is kept well in check, certainly with the roof down, the side window up and the optional wind deflector in place. With the hood up, wind noise, tyre roar and engine rasp are all well suppressed. And compared to the Lotus Elise, or even an MGF, refinement is extremely good. But the trade-off is that the Z3 doesn't possess Elise-type handling – the Lotus is kart-like, the 1.9 Z3 having a much softer, smoother, laid-back approach, so it is more saloon than sports.

The four-cylinder Z3 can be driven around corners quickly, but it isn't as much fun as the British cars. What the Z3 is never lacking is grip, even with standard 205/60 VR15 tyres (even more so with optional 225.50 VR16s, for example). So in terms of adhesion, the 1.9 Z3 can 'hang in there' longer than the majority of its rivals without losing grip. Essentially the four-cylinder Z3 is a secure and safe handler, if lacking the sporting prose of the Lotus.

Average fuel consumption is 35.8mpg (7.9ltr/100km), which can easily be improved upon over the touring route if driven sensibly. Just as well, as BMW hadn't been exactly generous with the tank size of 52ltr (11.2imp gal). This means that cruising along the motorway, a figure of 350-plus miles (560km) can be achieved before needing a refill, though considerably less in an urban environment.

The cabin of the 1.9 (without optional fitments such as chrome trim, leather and wood) is well made, but lacking in visual flair. Nevertheless, for a roadster the level of standard equipment is high, with power-steering, electric seat adjustment, electric windows and mirrors, all coming in the price. Try comparing this to an Elise! The same applies to the manually operated hood, the Lotus one being a nightmare to get up or down.

Really the Lotus and BMW are at different ends of the roadster rainbow. If you want a track-day special, but without the features and comfort to make everyday motoring enjoyable, you will have bought a Lotus Elise; whereas the Z3 1.9 won't perform as a track car, but will be brilliant for long- or short-haul journeys, with or without a passenger – and reliable too.

Road-Test Comment

Autosport's chief road-test editor Andrew Frankel summed up the situation perfectly in his *Driving Seat* column in the magazine's January 1996 issue:

What infuriated me about the Z3 was that every single person I spoke to who had driven it, felt differently about it. Some thought it the most electrifying small sports car they'd been in, while others considered that it failed to move the game materially on from the ground already masterfully occupied by the likes of the MGF and Alfa Spider. It was, depending on whom you spoke to, both thrilling and boring, ugly and attractive, inspired and cynically derivative.

The truth, as is usually the case – and this is also the author's opinion – is somewhere in the middle.

Pleasing the Majority

Compared to such narrow-focus machines such as the Lotus Elise, or even more so the Caterham Seven, the Z3 Series was intended to satisfy the needs of the majority in the roadster market. To start with, most of the people who criticize the car, in its various versions, either haven't actually driven one, or are journalists whose curiosity takes them no further than a few hours' acquaintance at a race-circuit launch or performance-oriented test session.

To appreciate what I mean, read a road test of the Lotus Elise, which almost always receives a five-star rating. But try actually living and owning one of the Lotus sportsters, and things are not quite so rosy: quite simply the Elise is one of the most uncomfortable cars of the modern era, with a strictly no-frills cabin and an engine derived from the

MGF (in other words, a 1.8 Rover lump). And then there is its unreliability, highlighted by *Top Gear*'s JD Power survey, in which the Elise came out very near the bottom of all the vehicles surveyed.

As another comparison, take the Japanese Honda S2000, for example: its performance is breathtaking, provided you keep within a power band of 6–9,000rpm. But try cruising in it, and it has less 'pull' than the most basic Civic hatchback.

By contrast, what the Z3 does, in all its guises, is provide a usable, everyday, comfortable drive with enough of the driving pleasures associated with roadsters to satisfy most people; only the extreme performance enthusiast is likely to be disappointed. Obviously this is with the proviso of model choice – and BMW had provided its customers with a fantastically wide choice (unlike the majority of its rivals), with everything from a sub-£20,000, 115bhp, four-cylinder budget version, right through to the barn storming 321bhp M Roadster costing twice as much. Yes, BMW made enough different Z3 models to satisfy virtually every taste and pocket.

The Production Z3 Arrives

So much for the reception the Z3 received. What most people would like to know now is what the actual car was like, and its technical specification. In this chapter I am looking purely at the four-cylinder entry models, as these were the first Z3s to go on sale.

The first concrete details of the forthcoming Z3 came in the summer of 1995, with official press photographs being made available in September that year. Its official launch came at the American Detroit Auto Show in January 1996. At that time the Stateside price of $25,000 was being quoted for the base 1.8 version, some $7,000 more than Mazda's MX-5 (known as the Miata in North America).

And the American market was all-important to the success of the Z3 – one of the major reasons for the car being built in South Carolina. With the Spartanburg plant geared up to build 30,000 Z3s a year, it was critical that demand should exceed supply: hence a competitive price. In Great Britain the price for a 140bhp 1.9 version (the 1.8 wasn't sold in Britain) was quoted at just under £20,000.

Comprehensive Specification

Traditionally, two-seat roadsters were spartan affairs, designed to concentrate exclusively on driving pleasure, but not including any features for those demanding creature comforts, since the latter were not deemed a priority. A Roadster in the pre-World War II era had no heater, little space (either for legs or stowage), and only the most rudimentary of weather protection. Even during the immediate post-war period things didn't improve much, and in truth virtually helped to 'kill off' the roadster type. Today, however, things are very different, as drivers expect both the thrill of open-top motoring and the creature comforts enjoyed by saloon-car drivers.

A major need in creating the Z3 was to cater for modern requirements, both from the comfort angle as well as those of safety/security; so the Z3 had to be not only fun, but well specified, too. Therefore even the most basic model enjoys features such as electrically operated seats (with manual backrest adjustment), windows and door mirrors, power steering, remote central locking, deadlocking and alarm activation, and even an RDS radio/cassette.

Safety wasn't overlooked, either, so all Z3s come with ABS anti-lock brakes, halogen headlamps, a third high-level brake light, side-impact protection and inertia-reel seat belts. There is a driver's airbag, impact cushion bumpers, and a headlamps-on buzzer.

Yes, the roadster owners of yesteryear would be truly amazed at the level of standard equipment and safety features that the Z3 series benefits from.

ABOVE: *The Z3 arrived in 1996 and is pictured that year (a 1.9 is shown), together with, in the background, left to right: 3/15 (1929), 315/1 (1935), 328 (1936), 507 (1956) and Z1 (1988).*

With the Z3, BMW set out to build a roadster that would have a much wider appeal than the specialist 507 and Z1 models that had gone before. The 1.9 version shown here cost around £20,000 ($35,000) when it went on sale during 1996 (1997 UK).

The Z3 is a car in which you can undertake much longer journeys than the average roadster, thanks to its saloon-car level of comfort, even with the hood down.

But right-hand-drive cars for UK customers were to be some twelve months behind the standard LHD version sold in North America and mainland Europe; and the long wait was to become a major embarrassment to the British importers, BMW GB.

It was, in fact, not until February 1997 that the first RHD Z3 1.9s were actually delivered to British customers; this came just weeks after the arrival in the UK of the film *Goldeneye*, in which James Bond used a four-cylinder Z3 in a cameo role. Maybe the new BMW roadsters screen time wasn't very long,

Some 3,300 customers had ordered one of the 1.9-litre Z3s before it finally reached Great Britain in RHD form during the spring of 1997.

The Z3 (a 1.9 was used) benefited hugely from the 1995 film Goldeneye, *starring Pierce Brosnan as secret agent 007 James Bond.*

but it certainly generated more publicity for the launch of a new car than at any time in the history of the automobile industry.

BMW's View

With a UK price span of £20,000–£40,000, the company saw itself as 'able to compete in all areas of the newly reborn roadster market'. BMW's official *UK Press Information* package, dated February 1997 (at the time of the 1.9 model's British launch) said:

> So what is BMW's view of the Roadster? Well, Z3 is classical in the sense that it has a front engine and rear-wheel drive, a long bonnet with a power bulge, and the familiar BMW kidney

grill, a steeply raked windscreen, a short round tail and smoothly flared wheel-arch fairings – the whole giving both a distinctive face and muscular body.

A Marketing Mistake?

Just why BMW chose to launch the Z3 in its four-cylinder 'economy' versions has to remain one of the industry's big questions. And there is no doubt that in terms of press reception, it was a bad move. A major problem was the arrival of the Porsche Boxster and Mercedes SLK. Unlike the new BMW design, these were, at the time, one-model cars and considerably more powerful and therefore more glamorous to the press than the 1.8 and 1.9 four-cylinder BMW Z3s (they were also considerably more expensive). Almost at once, questions were being asked as to the sense of BMW's decision not to take on the opposition right from the start. For example, in the January 1997 issue of *Complete Car*, journalist and motoring writer David Vivian (testing the new Z3 2.8 six) said what most thought: 'We can't help wondering what BMW could have done to its German rivals' perceived worth if it had hit them with the Z3 2.8 in the beginning.'

Four-Cylinder Power

Instead, BMW chose to launch its new roadster with either the 1.8 115bhp eight-valve, or 1.9 140bhp sixteen-valve, four-cylinder engines, manufactured in BMW's Austrian engine factory at Steyr.

Both these power units needed plenty of revs before anything meaningful began to happen. The chassis, on the other hand, was extremely competent, so the breathless performance of the four-cylinder (in both versions) was all the more irritating. Indeed, the whole car was quite obviously set up to cope with much more go – and this of course left everyone, most of all the press, wanting more power.

Underpowered the 1.8/1.9 four-cylinder Z3s may have been, but the cute yet macho looks, refined ride, safe handling and BMW badge still meant the base Z3s were highly desirable sportscars. This in turn led to high sales volumes.

Z3 1.9 Roadster (1996)

Engine	Liquid-cooled, sixteen valve, dohc inline, four valves per cylinder and variable length inlet pipes
Displacement	1,895cc
Bore	85mm
Stroke	83.5mm
Transmission	Five-speed, manual (four-speed automatic cost option)
Doors	Two
Seats	Two
Chassis	Unitary construction
Bodywork	Steel, galvanized, with bolt on panels
Suspension	Front: spring-strut front axle with anti-dive and anti-roll bar
	Rear: semi-trailing arm rear axle, anti-squat and anti-dive; anti-roll bar
Drive	Rear wheel
Wheels	Cast alloy 7.00 J × 15 front and rear
Tyres	205/60 VR-15 front and rear
Dimensions	
Overall length	4,025mm (159in)
Overall width	1,692mm (66in)
Overall height	1,288mm (51in)
Wheelbase	2,446mm (96in)
Dry weight	1,175kg (2,588lb)
Max power	140bhp @ 6,000rpm
Max torque	133lb ft (180Nm) @ 4,300rpm
Top speed	127mph (204km/h)
0–62mph (100km/h)	9.5sec

The Z3 1.9 had a displacement of 1,895cc (85 × 83.5mm). Its double overhead camshaft put out 140bhp, giving a top speed of 127mph (204km/h).

The sixteen-valve, 1.9litre, straight-four powerplant of the 1996–1999 Z3 1.9. Although producing 140bhp, it needed revs to give of its best. Maximum torque of 133lb ft (180Nm) was produced.

The 1.9 Litre Engine

Whereas the entry model 1.8 (1,796cc – 84 × 81mm) four-cylinder unit employed eight valves, the 1.9 (1,895cc – 85 × 83.5mm) came with sixteen-valve technology. Featuring twin overhead camshafts, four valves per cylinder, and variable length intake manifold pipes, the unit was based on what was found in the 318ti Compact and 318i Coupé.

The maximum power which was 140bhp at 6,000rpm, and maximum torque of 133lb ft (180Nm) at 4,300rpm, allowed the Z3 1.9 to accelerate from 0–62mph (0–100km/h) in 9.5sec, and in fourth and fifth gear from 50–75mph (80–120km/h) in 9.6 and 12.6sec. Its top speed was 127mph (204km/h).

An advantage of the four-cylinder engine over its six-cylinder brothers was most definitely fuel consumption, official BMW figures giving an average of 35.8mpg (7.9ltr/100km), as compared to 30.1mpg (9ltr/100km) for the 2.8 six. The touring route figures were 47.1mpg (6ltr/100km) and 38.2mpg (7.4ltr/100km), respectively.

Technical Innovations

Roller-type rocker arms were used for the first time by BMW: it was claimed that these significantly reduced friction between the camshaft and rocker arms. With roller-type arms the friction curve remains consistently low between idle speed and 6,000rpm, while the friction caused by conventional drag-type rocker arms is three times higher at 1,000rpm, and twice as high in the 6,000rpm range. Even with the engine idling, the new rocker arms allowed fuel economy to increase by some 6 per cent.

Reducing Friction
Both the cylinder head and valve drive had been updated in order to reduce friction and oscillating masses. Bucket tappets were introduced to operate in conjunction with the new

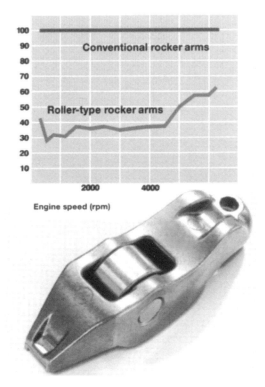

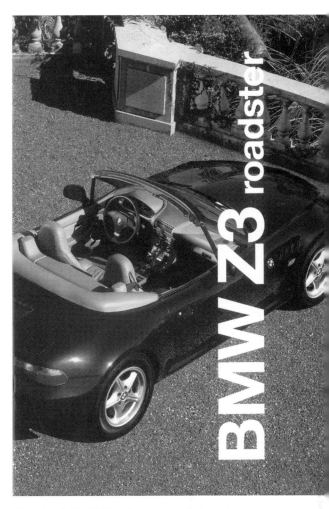

Roller-type rocker arms used on the 1.8/1.9 BMW Z3 series engines minimize friction between the rotating cams and the tappets, in fact reducing friction up to 60 per cent.

roller-type rocker arms. The fitment of conical valve springs, and a reduction in the size of the upper valve plate reduced oscillating masses by over 30 per cent, and the overall oscillating forces in the valve drive by around 15 per cent.

In addition, the camshaft mounts were cast in position, whilst the camshafts themselves featured cast-on balance weights as found on BMW's eight-cylinder engines.

Finally, the chain tensioning system (BMW no longer uses cam belts in any of its production engines) was improved throughout the engine speed range to minimize wear and increase service life. In total, due to all the above changes, the overall friction on the valve drive system was reduced by almost 70 per cent: a quite staggering figure. Not only did this give an improvement in fuel economy of 2.5 per cent, but it also helped in reducing noise levels and vibration.

The original 1996 Z3 brochure, now rapidly becoming a collectors' piece due to its rarity.

X-ray view of the four-cylinder Z3, showing the power-train layout, and the rear drive, and front and rear suspension systems.

Variable Inlet Manifolds

The 1.9 engine also benefited from BMW's individual control inlet manifold technology (DISA), providing variable manifold length to maximize torque at differing engine revolutions.

Digital Engine Management

The 1.9 Z3 engine benefited from the introduction of BMW's DME (digital motor electronics) M5.2 system, as found on BMW's twelve-cylinder engine. This electronic 'brain' consists of one single board, and provides sequential cylinder-specific fuel injection and precise fuel/oil metering. The greater benefits include:

- fuel economy;
- emission control;

- torque output;
- engine response;
- overall refinement;
- idle speed control;
- improved detection of misfiring to maximize the life of the catalytic converter.

DME M5.2 also comes with a high performance CAN (controller area network) database for fast and reliable communication with all other electronically controlled systems, such as ABS and ASC+7, thus further enhancing the overall reliability and efficiency of the car's performance.

Other Engine Features

The 1.9-litre engine also featured technical innovations of the 1.8-litre version. These

Z3 1.8 Roadster (1996)	
Engine	Liquid-cooled, eight-valve, dohc inline, four-cylinder
Displacement	1,796cc
Bore	84mm
Stroke	81mm
Compression ratio	9.7:1
Transmission	Five-speed, manual
Doors	Two
Seats	Two
Chassis	Unitary construction
Bodywork	Steel, galvanized, with bolt-on panels
Suspension	Front: spring-strut front axle with anti-dive and anti-roll bar
	Rear: semi-trailing arm rear axle, anti-squat and anti-dive; anti-roll bar
Drive	Rear wheel
Wheels	Steel, 6.50 J × 15 front and rear
Tyres	205/60 R15 91H front and rear
Dimensions	
Overall length	4,025mm (159in)
Overall width	1,692mm (66.6in)
Overall height	1,288mm (50.7in)
Wheelbase	2,446mm (96.3in)
Dry weight	1,250kg (2,533lb)
Max power	115bhp @ 5,500rpm
Max torque	124lb ft (168Nm) @ 3,900rpm
Top speed	120mph (194km/h)
0–62mph (100km/h)	10.5sec

included hot-film air-mass metering, adaptive knock control for each cylinder, duplex camshaft chain drive, and a stainless-steel exhaust manifold. In addition, fuel supply had been improved by the use of air-encapsulated injection valves with four-hole jets.

The increase in engine displacement from 1,796 to 1,895cc was achieved by increasing the cylinder bore size of the cast-iron block from 84 to 85mm, whilst the stroke was lengthened from 81 to 83.5mm. The actual length of the connecting rods themselves remained unchanged.

Getrag Gearbox
The five-speed manual gearbox was the familiar Getrag assembly from the 3 Series. This excellent box gave the 1.9 (and 1.8) Z3s a short, precise change, and was one of the car's best features (note: there was a different gearbox on the six-cylinder cars, with a stiffer action). The fifth gear features a direct 1:1 transmission ratio that provided a good balance between fuel economy and engine response.

The combination of a direct fifth ratio and a correspondingly lower rear-axle ratio enabled the propeller shaft to run more smoothly (with none of the drive shunt found on the Mercedes Benz SLK, for example). BMW specifies the use of AFT (automatic transmission fluid), made possible by the use of a two-mass flywheel that allows for smooth and easy gearshifts even in very cold weather. This fluid has the added advantage of only needing to be changed once every 60,000 miles (96,500km).

Automatic Transmission Option
With the Stateside market very much in its mind, even the four-cylinder Z3 1.9 was available with the cost option of an automatic gearbox. Unlike the six-cylinder 2.8 (later versions) and the 3.0-litre sixes, but not the M version, the four-cylinder Z3 has only ever been available in four-speed non-Steptronic form.

The four-speed automatic gearbox was the well tried device as used by the E36 3 Series, with electronic/hydraulic management, offering three driving programmes:

• E (economy): ensuring maximum economy by changing up gears early;
• S (sports): providing gear changes for maximum performance;
• M (manual): retaining gear engagement by the driver.

To minimize fuel consumption, the automatic transmission was provided with a converter lock-up clutch, providing direct flow of power to the rear axle. It is activated accordingly to the road speed in third and fourth gear to eliminate any slip in the converter. A built-in self-diagnostic system detects and records any defects. This transmission management system has a fail-safe programme, allowing the car to be driven to the nearest dealership. This automatic transmission also features a life-time only oil filling for the entire service life of the car. However, it is generally agreed that the auto transmission does not really suit the characteristics of the four-cylinder engine; it is much better when used with the six-cylinder powerplant.

The Chassis
Together with the styling, arguably the most important feature of a roadster is its chassis. BMW's answer with the Z3 was to provide it with a rigid steel monocoque, hot-galvanized on both sides, featuring a fully welded floorpan of high-strength steel plate to form a safe and durable cell (this type being known as 'unitary construction').

Dr Goeschel and his team of engineers paid considerable attention to ensuring that their new roadster provided a high level of both passive and active safety, as well as giving the driver a comfortable, yet sporting drive.

The Z3 Series, therefore, features an extremely strong passenger cell with pre-determined crumple zones front and rear, which allow low-cost sectional repair to the body in the event of even a medium-damage shunt. Side integral door reinforcements, combined with a high level of structural stability of the body, provide the Z3's occupants good protection from a side impact.

The following features were designed to minimize the risk of a side-impact collision:

- the stable, crosswise combination of ultra-strong A and B pillars, as well as side-sills;
- the crosswise connection to the floor-pan, bulkhead and rear cross-panel with the roof compartment;
- supports holding the doors on the side frame;
- a high-tensile overall structure provided by extra-strong door hinges and locks.

Together with the bonded laminated windscreen, the rigid tubular structure within the windscreen frame provides protection if the car should overturn.

As a result of the above features, the Z3 Series easily fulfilled all worldwide crash safety requirements, including the strict US legislative need for 35mph (56km/h) frontal collisions with full overlap (US-NCAP standard) and 55mph/88km/h (35mph/56km/h) offset frontal collision with 40 per cent overlap in accordance with the test conditions applied by the majority of Europe's leading automobile magazines.

The Z3 Body

Bolt-on Body Panels

The Z3 has been designed so that it can withstand low-speed bumps and be rebuilt more easily by featuring bolt-on panels. Up to 2.5mph (3.75km/h), front and rear collisions are absorbed by impact 'cushions' mounted behind the bumpers of the Z3, without any damage to the body. At higher speeds, up to 5mph (8km/h), the impact boxes absorb energy and can simply be cut out and replaced. In heavier impacts the Z3 still remains relatively simple to repair, since all panels forming the outer skin are bolted, then welded to make replacement easier, a concept pioneered by BMW with the Z1.

Galvanized Body Panels

Whilst the whole bodyskin of the Z3 is easily renewed in the event of damage, elaborate rust-proofing should keep the Z3 in a pristine state – significantly more so than the majority of yesteryear roadsters. Around 90 per cent of all the body panels are galvanized, then exposed to phosphate treatment and a cathode dip bath, and particularly exposed areas receive plastic coating and under-floor hollow cavity preservation treatment.

All the larger body panels are reinforced at predetermined points to insulate the occupants from undesirable vibration and resonance. Finally, to provide further refinement and reduce vibrations, two elastically connected anti-vibration weights in the rear bumpers oscillate with precisely the right counter-balancing effect to compensate for any torsional vibration from undulations in the road surface.

Drive and Handling

The Suspension System

In providing a relatively low centre of gravity, near 50/50 weight distribution, long-wheel base and taut suspension, Dr Burkhard Goeschel and his development team provided the Z3 Series with a car that was comfortable and provided safe handling characteristics. This is not as easy as it might sound, as it is one thing to create a fine-handling, single-purpose sports/racer, but altogether another when the requirement includes saloon-like comfort. Maybe the Z3 is not the best out-and-out sports car, but it certainly meets the dual challenges its design team were set.

Front Axle

The single-joint, McPherson spring-strut front axle found on the Z3 came straight from the 3 Series with only a slight increase in track and other relatively minor modifications. The anti-roll bar is connected to the transverse arm by a pendulum support that contributes to the Z3's good stability, but at the same time provides anti-dive characteristics.

Power-assisted rack-and-pinion steering, with a more direct transmission of 13.9:1 and elastic wheel-guidance joints, help provide light, precise, all-responsive steering. A three-spoke, albeit oversize steering wheel with airbag was fitted as standard equipment.

Rear Axle

A controversial design feature of the Z3 was its rear suspension layout. This was not the Z-type as used by the post-1990 3 Series saloon:

A BMW publicity shot of the four-cylinder Z3. Recognition points compared to its six-cylinder brothers included front spoiler, narrower track, and lack of small oblong parking/side lights on the outer sides of the front spoiler, and at the rear a single instead of twin exhaust outlet.

A Z3 1.9 with a particularly fearsome background – wouldn't fancy its chances if someone left the handbrake off!

instead the trailing-link type (like the E36 Compact) and was based on the old E30 saloon of the 1980s.

Many observers believe this to have been entirely on cost grounds, but this is in fact not true: actually a major reason was because the design team considered the older system better for its needs, with the Roadster's short rear overhang (and rear drive) combined with the need to provide adequate boot space (180ltr/6.3cu ft).

Although similar in design to the former M3 and E36 3 Series Compact, the rear track was actually 14mm (0.55in) wider than the Compact; in conjunction with re-tuned spring rates, firmer shock absorbers and an entirely new rear-axle mount, this gave superior handling to either the E30 M3 or the E36 Compact.

Fitted just forward of the rear axle, an integral plastic fuel tank has a capacity of 51ltr (11.2imp gal). This tank size is used throughout the Z3 range, including both the four-cylinder engine types.

A German-registered Z3 1.9 with the optional 16in five-star alloy wheels.

Braking Equipment

The four-cylinder Z3 models feature BMW's twin-circuit brake system using the ABS Mark IV anti-lock system as standard. The Mark IV type came with a three-channel control, incorporating four wheel-sensors and an electronic 'brain' for self-diagnosis.

Stopping power was provided by a quartet of solid discs measuring 286mm (11.26in) front, and 272mm (10.71in) rear. The handbrake being operated by additional drums on the rear wheels.

Wheels and Tyres

As standard, the Z3 1.9 was fitted with 7J × 15 Z-line aluminium wheels with 205/60VR-15V tyres; and the 1.8 steel disc-type wheels were fitted with 6.50J × 15 and 205/60HR-15 tyres. However, many owners specified a different wheel/tyre package in 15in, 16in or 17in sizes and wider tyres. But in all cases the spare remained the same, and suitable only as a short-term replacement until the original tyre could be repaired/renewed. This was a 3.5B × 15HZ tyre on a T125/90 steel rim.

Open–Top Motoring

On a dry, sunny day the Z3 offers the thrill of hood-down motoring – although thanks to the convenience and practicality of the soft-top roof, it also provides protection during the cold winter months. Operated by two levers at either side of the top windscreen frame, the soft top can be opened quickly and easily using a grab handle in the centre roof frame. When in the open position, the hood disappears completely into a recess in an area between the cabin and the boot. There is a moulded

With the hood down (manual operation standard on 1.8 and 1.9 four-cylinder models), a tonneau cover (shown) can be fitted. Many owners, however, tend to leave if off.

leatherette cover that can be fitted, but many owners simply do not bother with it, finding it a nuisance to fit and carry.

The six-cylinder models usually come with an electrically operated hood, and this could be ordered on the four-cylinder models as an optional extra. It is easy to use, although the car must be parked with the ignition on and the brake pedal depressed. A further point is that, unlike the Z8, for example, the catches must be opened and the hood pulled back a few inches and partly folded. Not difficult, but easy for a new owner to be puzzled as to why the hood won't go down when the buttons are pressed.

Another problem can be the hood's rear window, manufactured from green-tinted plastic (BMW call it 'polyacrylic glass'), as it will eventually become damaged due to scratches and the like. However, it can be simply

Rear light as fitted to all pre-2000 model year Z3s, including the four-cylinder cars. The M Roadster was the only version to retain this cluster after this time.

Unlike the M Series Z3 models, the four-cylinder version use this mirror type (shared by the 2.0, 2.2, 2.8 and 3.0 sixes). The M mirror is much rounder.

unzipped and a new 'window' installed relatively quickly and inexpensively. Should the entire roof need replacing, this can be done without drama since there is no glue connecting the roof bars to the soft top. Pre-2000 cars have a single lining; post-2000 cars feature a superior double-lined roof.

The Z3 Interior

The Cabin Area
The interior of the Z3 was designed to combine the essentials of the Roadster breed, meaning that instruments and controls were limited to the essentials, but with features that are required by the modern motorist.

In the four-cylinder models, cloth rather than leather was standard, in either flat-weave cloth upholstery, or BMW's new fabric Z-Tex, available as a no-cost option. Also available as a cost-only option were sports seats (leather only). Various colours for both cloth and leather could be specified.

Two arch-shaped inserts flow up from the cabin's central console and lead into the dash top: one houses the instrument cluster, and the other contains the optional passenger airbag. The air-outlet vents for demisting the side windows are integrated at the far right

and left. Beneath the vents and in the middle, black cylindrical ventilation nozzles, adjustable in all directions, ensure an adequate flow of air.

The Instrument Console
The instrument console itself is dominated by the tachometer and speedometer. These large, classically styled, white-on-black circular instruments are supported to right and left by a pair of smaller dials for coolant temperature and fuel gauge, respectively. Besides the instruments is a large push–pull switch (from the Compact) that operates the car's driving lights and fog lights, with an integrated dimmer control for the instrument panel illumination. The central console houses the heating/optional air conditioning, radio, ventilation controls, clock (or optional LC computer display), and additional switches such as electric roof, electric heated seats, and so on. The electric window switches lie on each side of the gear lever.

There is a lockable compartment (glovebox) and a small storage area between the seats (this is deleted if the optional Harmon Kardon Hi-Fi system is installed). Incidentally, the latter lockable 'box' is really only of use for a diary, maps or service documents.

ABOVE: A small lockable compartment between the two seats – its main use is for documents and the car's service record and handbook. However, in cars fitted with the optional Harmon/Kardon hi-fi loudspeaker system, this is deleted.

Instrument console found on the pre-2000 model four-cylinder range, plus 2.8 six. This car has optional equipment including electric hood operation, air conditioning, on-board computer and single disc CD player.

Non-Adjustable Steering Wheel

A feature of the cabin that has been roundly condemned is the non-adjustable, oversize steering wheel. However, I have never really found it a nuisance, as with the fully adjustable seats it is still possible to get very comfortable and to complete long distances without feeling restricted in any way. As for the rim size, it could do with being smaller, but it is something that I, for one, have learned to live with.

All the controls are light and easy to use. The pedals are slightly offset, but again I've used far worse, and you soon adapt to them. In fact, although quite bland, the Z3's cabin is generally

a good place to be. And its comfort cannot be faulted – as good as many saloons, in fact.

Engine and road noise are not a problem. Yes, there is more cabin noise than the average saloon, but it is never bad enough to stop you holding a conversation or listening to your favourite radio programme or CD. And having that open top on demand is a real bonus: with the side windows up and the wind deflector in place, the roof can come down even in the winter on a dry day. Put the heater control onto the footwell position and it is warm enough on the coldest day, too – and if you are lucky enough to have the optional heated seat package, that's even better!

A windbreak is one of the most important options in the Z3 'extras' list, since it drastically cuts down cabin turbulence.

BELOW: Chrome-line exterior items on the options list include this chrome ornamental grille.

Summary

Therefore, even the four-cylinder Z3s provide a good deal of fun, wind-in-the-hair motoring and ownership enjoyment. And their relatively low cost helped make the Z3 the second most popular roadster in the world (behind Mazda's MX-5 Miata). Yes, the six-cylinder models are even more fun, but they are also far more expensive, the M-version being twice as expensive as the 1.8. And owning a four-cylinder Z3 shouldn't be a painful experience, as not only is servicing less expensive than on the six-cylinder models, but fuel consumption can only be described as frugal: 40mpg (7l/100km) being easily obtainable whilst touring

There are also enough 'goodies' to make it possible to own your own 'special' Z3, even with the huge number around. When buying new, there was a three-year 60,000-mile (100,000km) warranty, which could be extended. And servicing isn't a problem thanks to BMW's comprehensive dealer network in most North American States and European countries. As already mentioned, there are more single-purpose sports cars, but very few that have all the benefits enjoyed by the Z3 Series. And the choice of models and the wide price range makes it easier for a greater range of potential owners to buy one than probably any other sports car. Bravo Z3!

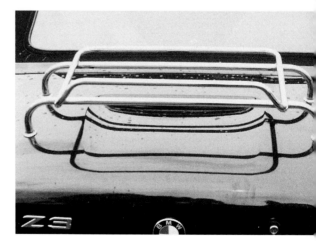

Another item from the options list is this boot-lid rack. BMW can also supply a matching lockable hard case. This latter item can be locked on the rack to protect it from theft.

Personalizing Your Z3

Many Z3 owners have personalized their car with accessories, like this 1.9 with AC Schnitzer body kit, exhaust and wheels.

It is possible to individually personalize your Z3, as the options list is truly vast, with equipment not only from BMW, AC Schnitzer and Alpina, but a whole army of aftermarket specialists. However, only the three companies mentioned come as factory 'approved'. Actually, trying to work out exactly what was 'standard' in any given year on a Z3 model is extremely difficult, as different markets often got entirely different specifications.

Factory-fitted options and standard equipment features included leather upholstery, automatic transmission, ASC&T (automatic stability control and traction), roll-over bars, larger alloy wheels, seat heating, air conditioning, cruise control, on-board computer, wood steering wheel, power hood, chrome-line interior and/or exterior, various radios, and metallic paint.

Items that can be purchased and fitted by the dealer include a colour-coded hard top, CD autochanger, folding wind deflectors, a rear luggage rack with special case (maximum load 30kg/66lb), and 'speedster humps' behind the headrests – plus various AC Schnitzer and Alpina styling products.

These are just a selection; the full list would require a book almost by itself!

A vast selection of alloy wheel upgrades exist for the Z3, ranging from 15 to 18in. Probably the best wheel size, certainly for the four-cylinder models, is 16in.

6 Six Appeal

'Power. It's what separates the winners from the wannabes' as one American journalist summed up the new 2.8 version of the Z3, compared to its four-cylinder brothers in a 1997 road test. And he was quite right: whilst the Z3 had proved an indisputable sales and image-building success, there were many who yearned for more performance.

But with their new six-cylinder model, BMW engineers hadn't simply put in a bigger cube engine and fitted fatter rubber: instead, with the 2.8 it was very much a case of uprating the car. Costing $35,900 Stateside, the Z3 2.8 arrived in the UK in August 1997, just in time for the new 'R' registration prefix, with a price tag of £28,115.

ABOVE: Proclaimed by many, including the author, as the best of the Z3 Series, the 2.8 arrived in the UK during August 1997, just in time for the new 'R' registration prefix. It had gone on sale in the rest of the world, including Germany, a few months earlier.

Compared to the original four-cylinder cars, the new 2.8 six was a revelation. Not only did it have much more power (193bhp) but the six-cylinder car also had a much higher specification (UK), including electric hood, leather, 16in alloy wheels, on-board computer, traction control, and limited slip differential. Note that this car is fitted with optional roll-over bars at extra cost.

This 1998 Z3 2.8 has chrome pack additions including mesh grilles, door handles, windscreen frame and chrome Z-star alloy wheels.

The changes, as compared to the existing four-cylinder version, included more power, wider track, larger/wider tyres, revised suspension, revised body traction control, limited slip differential, a stronger gearbox, more powerful brakes and a whole host of extra equipment. Yes, this wasn't just a revamped engine, it was virtually a redesign.

The Six-Cylinder Engine

At the heart of the newcomer was a light-weight 158kg (348lb), all-aluminium, twenty-four-valve, straight six-cylinder engine, already familiar to drivers of the 328, 528 and 728 saloons.

Displacing 2,793cc (84 × 84mm), this engine put out 192bhp at 5,300rpm, and 203lb ft (275Nm) of torque at 3,950rpm. Impressive though these statistics were, they only told half the story, since BMW's innovative VANOS variable valve timing enhanced torque delivery, and thereby flexibility, at much lower engine speeds: 80 per cent of maximum torque being available at 1,500rpm, little more than idling speed!

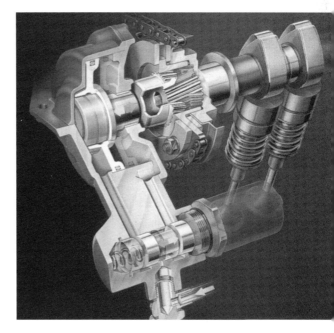

Variable camshaft control (VANOS). Masterminded by DMW (Digital Motor Electronics), this adjusts the inlet camshaft hydro mechanically as a function of engine speed and the position of the accelerator pedal. The result is much improved engine torque. Early 2.8 (pre-2000 model year) came with single VANOS (shown). Post-2000 cars have double VANOS.

Road-Testing the Z3 2.8

In the author's opinion the 2.8 is the best Z3 there is. Why? Well, to start with, it has a peach of an engine, the example tested being a 1998 single VANOS model with the original body shell (later 2.8s, before the introduction of the 3.0, having double VANOS and the revised body).

The straight-six engine (from the 328, 528 and 728 saloons) is an all-aluminium unit that is both super smooth and deliciously torquey (80 per cent being produced from a mere 1,500rpm). And because the engine extends further back in the engine compartment, the 2.8's front/rear weight distribution is the optimum 50/50 balance, and actually an improvement over the four-cylinder Z3's 52/48 per cent.

Compared to the 1.8/1.9 models, the 2.8 gained a wider track, wider tyres (16in standard, 17in optional), ASC+T traction control, and a 25 per cent locking rear differential (like the M Roadster). These, combined with the superior weight distribution, and power enough to make use of the Z3's grip levels, makes the 2.8 much more relaxing and enjoyable to drive, whether fast or slow.

As soon as you fire that six-cylinder engine into life you know this is going to be fun. But unlike the M version – or even the 3.0 – the 2.8 is so undemanding, even when making full use of the 192 horses under the bonnet. The 2.8 is also a smooth operator compared to its bigger, more powerful brothers.

Driving the 2.8, you soon realize that here is the ideal Z3: enough power to enjoy yourself, a level of smoothness to make you enjoy the longest of journeys, safe and strong brakes, and just the right balance of power for the chassis.

On the down side, the car I tested had the manual gearbox, the same unit as in the M version. However, unlike the box fitted to the smaller models, working up through this one requires considerable effort of the driver – it simply is not the hot-knife-through-butter operation of the Getrag unit found in the four-cylinder models (and also in the 2.0 and 2.2 sixes). As such it is the only really weak point in the 2.8, even though down-shift quality is fine. And as the 2.8 is such a superb cruiser, it is also ideally suited to the automatic gearbox option (unlike the four-cylinder versions).

The real joy of the 2.8 is the ease with which it will travel both fast and slowly; and best of all is its consummate ability on the climbs and descents of all those twisty bits. On the faster corners you adopt a smooth flowing style, but on the real slow hairpin-type bends you can have the best fun, the tyres chirruping in protest as you nail 200bhp through the rear wheels and are able to feed the back end out in a fully controllable manner. Somehow doing the same thing in the more powerful versions simply isn't quite as easy. Yes, they have more power, but the 2.8 has just enough power for the job at hand.

The engine also fully plays its part in making the 2.8 the best cruiser in the Z3 family. Thanks to its silken smooth, fuel-injected motor – which seems to be almost completely free of vibration – the 2.8 provides a superb long-distance drive. Yes, I know there are also the 2.0 and 2.2 sixes, but these don't possess the 2.8's torque figures.

The standard 16in, 225-section tyre package is best, as it gives enough grip, but not too much to stop the fun, and at the same time cuts down on the road noise as compared to some of the larger/wider tyre sizes available as options.

Fuel consumption on long runs can also be impressive, with well over 40mpg (7ltr/100km) possible with care on the touring route.

All in all, the 2.8 gets my vote as the best Z3. What a pity, therefore, that BMW axed it from the range in favour of the bigger 3.0.

Performance Figures

In real road-driving terms this means the 2.8 version accelerates from 50 to 75mph (80 to 120km/h) in fourth and fifth gears in 6.5 and 8.9 seconds, respectively. Maximum speed is 139mph (224km/h). Weighing in at 1,335kg (2,944lb) dry, the new six-cylinder model could accelerate from 0–62mph (0–100km/h) in a little under 7sec. Not only this, but with an average of 29.1mpg (9.7ltr/100km) over the new EU cycle, it was frugal too, considering its performance potential.

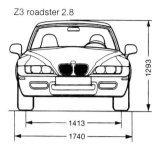
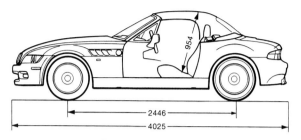
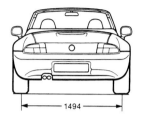

Z3 roadster 2.8

1293

1413
1740

954

2446
4025

1494

All dimensions in mm.
Luggage compartment capacity 165 litres/5.8 cu ft (to the VDA standard).

Three-view set of BMW drawings showing dimensions (in mm) for the 1998 model year Z3 2.8 model.

Chester enthusiast Ian Davis taking delivery of his brand-new, high-spec Z3 2.8 on 1 August 1998. He had waited eighteen months since placing his order. With features such as air conditioning, additional chrome trim, purple Oregon leather and Z-star alloys, it cost £32,500.

Shoehorning in BMW's inline six-cylinder engine meant there is a distinct lack of room under the bonnet. This meant relocating the battery into the boot, adjacent to the spare wheel.

A Fine Handling Car

In creating its first six-cylinder Z3, BMW engineers were able to achieve the ideal 50/50 front-to-rear weight distribution, as compared to the figures for the four-cylinder versions, namely 52/48. This, combined with a wider track (+ 2mm front +67mm rear vs Z3 1.9) and firmer, more sporting suspension, dropping everything by 20mm, created a fine handling car. The newcomer also benefited from the addition of a limited slip differential (with a 25 per cent lock-up ability), and a switchable ASC+T anti-slip control system. Due to the space taken by the six-cylinder power unit, the battery location was transferred from the engine compartment to the boot.

Improved Stopping Power

Braking had been improved by fitting ventilated brake discs up front in response to the extra power and added weight of the six cylinder power plant. And of course, as with the 1.8/1.9 models, ABS was a standard fitment. This then ensured the 2.8 stopped as well as it went.

A New Look

At the first glance of the long bonnet, small tail and steeply raked windscreen, one could have been forgiven for thinking the 2.8 was the same car as the 1.8/1.9-litre cousin. However, a closer look would have revealed that the 2.8 six was distinguished by a new front apron with larger air dam, fog lights and small oblong side lights, while at the rear there were more muscular wheel arches, adding 86mm (3.4in) to the width of the car, and twin exhaust pipes. The 16in instead of 15in tyres, and the electrically operated hood (both standard equipment on the UK model), rounded off the exterior

---

The Z3 2.8 Roadster (1997)

Engine	Liquid-cooled, twenty-four valve, dohc, inline, six-cylinder with single VANOS and Digital Motor Electronics (DME)
Displacement	2,793cc
Bore	84mm
Stroke	84mm
Compression ratio	10.2:1
Transmission	Five-speed, manual, all synchromesh gearbox
Doors	Two
Seats	Two
Chassis	Unitary construction
Bodywork	Steel, galvanized, with bolt-on panels
Suspension	Front: spring-strut front axle with anti-dive and anti-roll bar
	Rear: semi-trailing arm rear axle, anti-squat and anti-dive; anti-roll bar.
Drive	Rear wheel
Wheels	Cast alloy 7J × 16 front and rear
Tyres	225/50 VR-16 front and rear

Dimensions

Overall length	4,025mm (158.5in)
Overall width	1,740mm (68.5in)
Overall height	1,293mm (50.9in)
Wheelbase	2,446mm (96.3in)
Dry weight	1,335kg (2,944lb) manual, 1,375kg (3,032lb) automatic
Max power	192bhp @ 5,300rpm
Max torque	203lb ft (275Nm) @ 3,950pm
Top speed	139mph (223.6km/h) manual, 137mph (221km/h) automatic
0–62mph	6.9 seconds manual, 7.2 seconds automatic

ABOVE: The 2.8 has electric hood operation as standard…

However, it is necessary not only to release the two levers (located next to the sun visors), but also to lift and fold the hood as shown, before electric operation takes over.

differences between the existing fours and their new six-cylinder offspring.

It was much the same story within. The creature comforts of the 2.8 as standard included not only items found in the earlier models, such as radio/cassette, electric windows, seat adjustment and mirrors, remote central locking with deadlock, power-assisted steering and driver airbag – but new toys such as leather upholstery, on-board computer and electric hood operation.

The Z3 Series features unitary chassis construction, however the main body panels are bolted on, making replacement, if needed, much easier and cheaper.

BELOW: Electric seat adjustment (forward/backwards) and for height is standard on all six-cylinder models, including the 2.8.

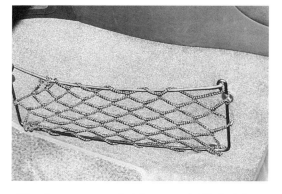

Leather is standard for the 2.8 (plus the other six-cylinder models). The wood steering wheel is a cost option.

Although mats are a standard fitment on all Z3s (both four- and six-cylinder models), this useful oddments holder is a cost option (located in the passenger's footwell).

Cam covers and oil filler plug of the 2.8-litre BMW inline six-cylinder engine.

M Sport chrome gear lever as fitted to the 2.8 model.

But No Badge...

On the original Z3 models, BMW's designers had resisted the temptation to adorn their new model with boastful badgework – not even a demure chrome '2.8' emblem to tell the world that here was something different to the lower power versions. Instead, it was left to the knowledgeable to spot the differences and so know the truth. Actually, considering all the saloons are badged, the company's policy seemed strange; particularly as, from 1999 onwards, the Series Two 2.8 (double VANOS), and later the new 3.0 version, were both been given chrome badges (sited near the boot-lid release).

Comparisons are Made

Obviously, comparisons were soon being made regarding the 2.8's ability as compared to its perceived opposition - the Porsche Boxster and Mercedes-Benz SLK. Whilst it was generally agreed that the 2.8 was much superior in terms of performance to the Merc, it was a closer run thing with the Porsche. In fact as a pure sports car the Stuttgart-built flat six usually came out on top. However, the BMW scored over the Boxster in areas such as price, equipment levels, mid-range punch and comfort. Of course these comparisons were made during 1997 and 1998, before BMW and Porsche brought out the 3.0 and Boxster S, respectively.

Press Comments

When it was launched in 1997, the Z3 2.8 was generally well received by the world's motoring press – in fact it had a much better reception than that given to the 1.8/1.9 versions. *Car Magazine*, when compiling its top ten cars, including the Z3 2.8, commented: 'God only knows how they'll sell any 1.9 jobs when this hits the showrooms. Well worth the wait.'

As a matter of interest the other nine cars were the Subaru Impreza Turbo; Peugeot 106 GTi; Lotus Elise; Jaguar XK8; Volkswagen

The 2.8 (1996–1999 version) in single VANOS form produces 192bhp at 5,300rpm, and 203lb ft (275Nm) of torque at 3,950rpm. It can propel the car to 139mph (224km/h); the 0–62mph (0–100km/h) acceleration figure is 6.9sec (7.2sec auto version).

Passat; Renault Megane Scenic; Ford Ka; BMW 528; and the Ferrari F355.

Press comments were extremely favourable right across the board:

> It would be easy to expect a compromise in the process; get some things, give up some things, but the six-cylinder engine and other enhancements that make a Z3 into a Z3 2.8 are all genuine improvements, and do nothing to diminish the package's basic goodness. If speed costs money, then it is value received for dollar invested.
>
> *Road & Track*

> The Z3 2.8 is a real sports car by comparison. Compared to the SLK (Mercedes), it is more enjoyable to drive fast, it is quicker off the line, and it makes the right kind of noises. We'd have said the same things about the BMW 507 in the fifties, too, compared with the 190SL.
>
> *Automobile Magazine*

The 2.8 has power enough not only to make it a serious performance car, but the smoothness and flexibility of the engine make it an excellent touring cruiser.

LEFT: *Optional chrome-line 16in Z-star BMW alloy wheel. UK price (1998) including taxes, £334.87 (per wheel).*

BELOW LEFT: *Roll-over bars, cost option UK price (1998) £720, including taxes.*

BELOW: *385mm diameter, maple wood steering wheel, another cost option extra, cost (1998) £415, including taxes.*

The straight six pushes the BMW Z3 into the lead. The Z3 roadster has been transformed by BMW's straight six. Andrew Frankel discovered it has grunt to match its looks.

Motor Sport

With their new concoction called the Z3 2.8, BMW engineers have taken the Carrol Shelby approach to roadster design. Stuff in a high-performance powerplant, plaster on some beefy rubber, and let action begin.

Motor Trend

One long straight is like a rumpled carpet. The Z3 (2.8) is impressively smooth over this, even at around 90mph [150km/h].

Autocar

I'd have my Z3 stripped of all the options, windbreak included, if it meant that I could afford the 2.8 litre engine. The engine really makes the car, giving it the character it lacks with the four-cylinder engine.

Autocar

The BMW Z3 2.8: A Passenger's View
By Rita Welsh

I have never been particularly interested in sports-type cars. Previously I thought 'Why have a car like that? You can't see the view, can't carry luggage and family, can't go any faster than the speed limit!' However, a recent spin from Edinburgh to the north of Scotland with the author in his Z3 2.8 changed my mind.

The car's road-holding ability made Scottish hairpin bends into easy curves. The powerful engine levelled out the hills, and the quiet ride made conversation a pleasure, even with the roof down – yes, we do get weather for that in Scotland! Surprisingly, the aerodynamic design of the windscreen and the optional mesh screen behind the seats reduced air disturbance to a minimum, thus doing away with the need for warm coats and hats on a sunny day.

The seat, once finely adjusted, gave good support and was comfortable, and the wide windscreen and large side windows offered good views of the surrounding landscape. In town, the build of the bonnet made the car seem larger and higher off the road than it actually is – and I felt less intimidated by larger vehicles than I had expected.

Although the boot space is small, it is still large enough to take two weekend bags, jackets and boots for the Scottish summer climate, and to accommodate accumulated souvenirs on the return journey. In addition, the surprisingly economic fuel consumption – approximately 38mpg [7ltr/100km] over the 550-mile [885km] round trip – would please any canny Scot.

The only drawback of the Z3 is the attention it attracts. It acts like a 'red rag to a bull' to so many other drivers – for some reason they cannot sit behind us on the road, but have to try to overtake or out-manoeuvre us in much less able motors. Again, the Z3 proves its worth in the hands of a good driver. The powerful engine pulls easily away from trouble, the handling and road-holding allows responsive manoeuvring, and the reliable brakes ease the car back to a safe distance from reckless overtaking by other vehicles.

To sum up: if you want views over the roadside hedges, go by bus. If you want to take children, dogs and luggage, go by estate car. But if you want to enjoy the air, the views, the comfort and the exhilarating driving experience – then catch a lift in a Z3 on a sunny summer's day in Scotland.

Summary

Hailed as the ultimate Z3 when it was launched back in 1997, the 2.8 is sadly no longer available on the new car market; nevertheless, it remains probably the most convincing variant of the BMW Z3 family. It manages to be sports car, cruiser, comfort wagon; it is value for money, being frugal on fuel and reliable on service; and it is even relatively cheap to insure and maintain.

Yes, there are faster Z3s, more frugal Z3s, but none with such a wide range of abilities – and that's what makes it number one in my book.

The view that most other road users see of the Z3 2.8 when in full performance mode.

7 The M Roadster

When it made its debut in 1997, the M3-powered M Roadster was the fastest-accelerating production car BMW had ever built (0–62mph (100km/h) in 5.4sec).

When BMW revealed the prototype of the 3.2-litre Z3M Roadster at the 1996 Geneva Show, the Munich-based company completed its new roadster family. If the 1.8/1.9 four-cylinder models represented the Z3 in its most simple, affordable mode, and the 2.8 six as the cruiser, then the M version has got to be the performance sports car.

The M version might have weighed in at 165kg (364lb) more than the Z3 1.9, but at 1,350kg (2,977lb) it was still 100kg (220lb) lighter than an M3 Coupé. This meant that performance was electric, with a 0–62mph (0–100km/h) figure of 5.4sec, at the time of the launch making it the fastest-accelerating BMW production car yet. Despite poor aero-dynamics – a best Cd of 0.41 with the hood erect – there was more than enough power to require BMW to electronically limit maximum speed to 155mph (250km/h), almost 20mph (32km/h) faster than the 2.8 version.

Without a doubt the star feature of the Z3M was its engine, which is described below and provided the latest version of the Z3 roadster theme with its abundance of muscle and firepower.

The Z3M Powerplant

It almost goes without saying that BMW had to create their M version of the Z3 Roadster. In the M3 engine it had one of the world's finest powerplants, which also had the distinc-

tion of breaking the 100bhp/litre barrier, the holy grail of the auto industry.

The Engine

Displaying 3,201cc (86.4 × 91mm), the M3 engine developed a whopping 321bhp @ 7,400rpm (note, the American market engine 'only' puts out 240bhp) and is one of the most powerful normally aspirated engines on the planet. And it's not just about outright power, as the M3 has maximum torque figures of 258lb ft (350Nm) at 3,250rpm. This makes it an exceedingly flexible drive, with immense pulling power from a mere 2,000rpm, continuing all the way up to 7,600rpm.

The Z3M Roadster (1997): Specification

Engine	Liquid-cooled, twenty-four–valve, dohc, inline, six-cylinder with double VANOS and Digital Motor Electronics (DME)
Displacement	3,201cc
Bore	91mm
Stroke	86.4mm
Compression ratio	11.3:1
Transmission	Five-speed, manual, all synchromesh gearbox
Doors	Two
Seats	Two
Chassis	n/a
Bodywork	Steel, galvanized, with bolt-on panels
Drive	Rear wheel
Wheels	Front 7.5J × 17in
	Rear 9J × 17in
Tyres	Front 225/45 ZR-17 run-flat type
	Rear 245/40 ZR-17 run-flat type
Dimensions	
Overall length	4,050mm (159in)
Overall width	1,858mm (73in)
Overall height	1,288mm (51in)
Wheelbase	2,459mm (97in)
Dry weight	1,350kg (2,977lb)
Max power	321bhp @ 7,400rpm
Max torque	258lb ft (350Nm) @ 3,250rpm
Top speed	155mph (250km/h), limited
0–62mph	5.4sec
(European model specifications quoted)	

The 321bhp M3 Evolution engine of the M Roadster not only provides phenomenal torque and performance, but also manages to do it with the minimum of fuel.

On the road, this means the European Z3M has exceptional power and torque at its disposal. For example, in fifth (top) gear, acceleration from 50 to 75mph (80 to 120km/h) takes only 7sec, whilst in fourth it takes just 5.3sec; and this virtually seamless progress is only halted when the electronic rev limiter kicks in to restrict the top speed to 155mph (250km/h).

The MS S 50 Digital Motor Electronics
The 3.2 M power unit featured the first engine management system ever developed by BMW in-house, the MS S 50 Digital Motor Electronics. This system was the result of joint development by BMW and electronics specialists

Displacing 3,201cc (86 × 91mm), the M3 Evo power unit has maximum torque figures of 250lb ft (350Nm) at 3,250rpm.

The 3.2M power unit featured the first engine management system developed by BMW in-house, the MS S 50 DME (Digital Motor Electronics).

Siemens, and offered the Munich company a new kind of engine management philosophy with more veracity and intelligence than conventional systems, and with the advantage of being exclusively tailored to BMW's M models. Conventional systems control idle air supply by a bypass adjuster in the throttle butterfly manifold; the new BMW electronic system, however, incorporated a programmable, cylinder-specific injection time adjustment function, which synchronized the fuel/air mixture in each individual cylinder.

The MS S 50 system also had the advantage of ease of maintenance, and was capable of self-diagnosis; it offered overrun control, constantly supervising the oil level and acting as an immobilizer by interrupting the injection of fuel. Thus it met the special needs of the high-performance M powerplant better than a bought-in assembly would have been able to. At the same time it featured existing benefits of conventional systems, such as solid-state distributors, hot-film air mass metering, and integrated, adaptive knock control. So whenever RON 98 premium unleaded fuel is not available, the M engine can be run on RON 95.

MS S 50 features may be summarized as:

- high performance software operating at twenty million calculations per second;
- optimized enrichment of fuel/air mixture when accelerating;
- cylinder-specific ignition timing, ignition period and knock control;
- all control functions of double VANOS operating at extremely high adjustment speed; fuel pump switches off as a safety function in the event of a crash.

The Crankcase and Crankshaft

The crankcase of the M engine was manufactured from grey cast iron; the crankshaft was forged from high strength steel and came with seven main bearings and twelve counterweights. Working with a vibration damper, this allows engine speeds up to 7,600rpm. The main bearing shells on the crankshaft measure 20mm in width and have an inner diameter of 60mm. The big-end shells are 18mm wide with an inner diameter of 49mm.

Connecting Rods and Pistons

The connecting rods of the M3 engine are sintered, meaning they are manufactured in one piece and cracked to form a perfect, strong and unique fit when the two halves are connected to the crankpin. With its bearing bush in place, the small-end opening of the con-rod measures 21mm in diameter, with the big-end opening measuring 49mm across.

The M Series' pistons feature four valve pockets on their crown – two each for the inlet and exhaust valves. These pistons feature graphite-coated sides to reduce noise and friction, and are designed to run on RON 98 premium fuel (unleaded). The minimum requirement is RON 95 (unleaded). Compression ratio is 11.3:1, and the pistons are cooled by oil spray jets fitted in the crankcase, a method more commonly known as piston floor cooling.

The Cylinder Head and Valve Gear

Operating according to the cross-flow principle, the two-piece cylinder head was designed for very high thermal and mechanical loads. The combustion cycle is fed through four valves per cylinder, the valve drive incorporating twin overhead camshafts, and valve adjustment being maintained by hydraulic compensators.

The combustion chambers as well as the inlet and outlet ports are specially finished for optimum gas flow, as well as maintaining minimal emissions and thus pollution.

The cylinder-head gasket, made from asbestos-free material, does not need to be retightened and is thus maintenance free. The valve casing and cylinder head feature additional oilways to improve flow on fast bends, a feature that is necessary in such a high performance car where the driver may push it to the limit on frequent occasions.

The twin overhead camshafts are manufactured of shell-cast, heat-treated steel and run in seven bearings, and they open the valves through an angle of no less than 260 degrees. The camshafts are driven directly from the crankshaft via a duplex roller chain.

Because of the engine's sporting nature and high performance, the valves are specially designed and made of high temperature-resistant steel. The exhaust valves are sodium-filled for enhanced temperature resistance. All twenty-four valves are operated by lightened cup tappets, and each valve has progressive double valve springs. This results in an extremely light valve-drive system, thus assisting higher engine revolutions than would otherwise be possible.

Double Variable Camshaft Adjustment (Double-VANOS)

The M engine benefited from BMW's Double-VANOS: developed jointly by BMW and BMW's M Sport Division, this is a control unit that adjusts the camshaft infinitely and automatically throughout the entire engine or rev speed range. Reacting to the throttle butterfly opening angle and engine speed, it sets the intake and exhaust camshafts to their optimum position. Then, by permanently monitoring the position points of the reference wheels on the camshafts, the control unit is able to constantly supervise the relative angle of the intake and exhaust camshafts.

It compares actual with target data, and if necessary, resets each camshaft position by means of four hydraulic control valves. The 100bar oil pressure required to control the

Double VANOS

All the M Series engines benefit from BMW's double VANOS variable camshaft control. VANOS is an abbreviation of 'Viable Nockenwellen Spreizung' (meaning 'variable camshaft adjustment'). This system eliminates the usual compromise between the need for both increased torque and increased top-end power. Conventional wisdom indicates that one is usually sacrificed for the other – double VANOS defeats this notion by continually adjusting the duration of the inlet and exhaust camshafts for both increase torque at low engine revolutions and optimum power at the top end of the rpm scale.

The reduction in unburned residual gas also improves the idling qualities of the power unit, and special control maps for the warm-up phase enhance the efficiency of the catalytic converter.

The M Roadster (and certain other Z3 models) benefits from the BMW double-VANOS variable camshaft control system. This provides exceptional torque figures, as it increases engine flexibility throughout the rev range.

Besides the M Series, other Z3 models to benefit from double-VANOS were the 2.0-, 2.2- and 3.0-litre cars, plus the later (post-1999) 2.8 series. The earlier 2.8s feature single VANOS.

camshaft is generated by an oil pump. This is driven by the exhaust camshaft, allowing a very high control speed of 250 milliseconds for the maximum adjustment of the crank angle.

The Cooling System

To ensure the engine maintains optimum temperature, BMW developed a very sophisticated cooling system. This featured a ring-slide thermostat flanged onto the water pump from above, keeping the temperature of the coolant at a constant level, both when idling and at high engine speeds. During the cooling process the water pump works efficiently, circulating 270ltr (59.4imp gal) of coolant per minute at 7,000rpm.

The Exhaust System

Manufactured of high quality stainless steel, the two-piece exhaust manifold has no welding spots or unsightly seams, thereby ensuring both high quality and a high service life expectancy. There are two turn pipes at the rear of the exhaust system.

The catalyst system is divided into two metal chambers housing four tri-metal-coated monoliths. Each exhaust pipe is monitored by two oxygen sensors fitted inside the main manifold pipes and operating in stereo mode. The advantages of this system include low exhaust counter-pressure, and rapid warm-up after the engine has been started from cold.

To reduce exhaust emissions of the M engine to an even lower level, it comes with secondary air injection. When the engine is started from cold, air is injected via a special pump directly into the cylinder head behind the exhaust valves. This serves to 'oxidize' the exhaust gases before they enter the catalytic converters which would not yet be at their normal operating temperature of 300°C. The result is a reduction in the hydrocarbon emissions and an increase in exhaust temperature, thus speeding up the warming process of the converters. Once the converters have reached normal working temperature, the MS S 50 engine management system switches off the secondary injection process.

The M Roadster Gearbox

Unlike the M3 saloon, the M Roadster (and Coupé) have to make do with five, not six gears; this is because there is simply not enough room for the M3's usual six-speed transmission. In its place comes the five-speed box from the 2.8 (and its replacement, the 3.0) Z3, featuring synchromesh on all gears. Top gear ratio is 1:1, giving a good compromise between performance and fuel economy.

Flywheel Mass

A further feature of the M engine is the wide-angle, two mass flywheel without oil damping. An additional weight-optimized flywheel is matched up with a 240mm-diameter, single-plate diaphragm, hydraulically spring-operated clutch. This helps provide positive gear changes without any undesirable drive-system vibration.

Summary

So that is the technical side of the Z3M Roadster's powerplant, and a fuller appreciation of its capacity should help explain why this engine is capable of such outstanding on-road performance, whilst at the same time retaining a level of sophistication not usually found in such a vehicle. This is what makes this engine the true classic it is: power, sophistication and reliability.

The M Roadster Chassis

The M Sport Division's task in building the M Roadster was obviously not simply a case of stuffing in the 3.2 litre 321bhp motor from the M3 saloon; that would have been asking just too much of the basic Z3 design. Instead it carried out a number of important improvements to areas such as suspension, brakes, wheels, tyres and the like. It also had to work along with the original Z3 concept of the comfortable, practical, everyday roadster – so, like the rest of the series, the M Roadster was to be a far cry from the harshness of yesteryear sports cars.

The Suspension

The M Roadster boasts a single-joint spring strut with displaced castor, a small positive steering roll, compensation of transverse forces and anti-dive. This gave it almost the same configuration as the M3 Saloon, with independent suspension on track control arms and McPherson struts, although the combination was tuned to meet the requirements of the new high performance roadster.

Although much criticized by the press, the semi-trailing arm, rear-axle design had *not* been employed by BMW on its E30 3 Series, but on the former M3 racing car. For the smaller-engined Z3s it had in any case been improved over its original saloon-car layout. For its application on the M Roadster, layout had been further updated with a number of major changes.

It now came with a stronger axle sub-frame and reinforced semi-trailing arms, as well as firmer, tauter anti roll-bars, dampers and springs. This new sub-frame, redesigned to accommodate the modified final drive, features a transmission ratio of 3.15:1.

The shock-absorber damper units of the M Roadster are firmer and tauter than the other Z3 models; in addition the damper springs are considerably harder (but tighter). Together with modified wheel geometry, new stub-axle

The Z3 M Roadster features an uprated chassis and stiffer suspension (with shorter springs) than the other, less powerful Z3 Roadsters.

kinematics and reinforced plate-springs, they combine to offer the suspension characteristics best suited to the requirements demanded by the M Roadster's higher performance potential.

Unlike the smaller-engined Z3s, the M version has no electronic traction control. Instead, like the 2.8 (and 3.0) versions, it features limited slip differential, offering 25 per cent locking action to ensure everything is as well mannered as is possible in a car with over 320bhp being put out via the rear wheels. BMW reasoned that the M version would be purchased by knowledgeable and experienced drivers, and so it could leave out the normal traction-control devices.

Steering

Like its smaller Z3 brothers, the M Roadster features rack-and-pinion steering with hydraulic servo assistance and a transmission ratio allowing some 3.2 turns of the steering wheel from lock to lock. This, of course, cannot be considered as quick steering: for example, the front-wheel-drive, Alfa Romeo GTV/Spider provides a ratio of 2.8. The M version of the Z3 features a smaller diameter (but still non-adjustable) steering wheel than the smaller-engined models.

The Braking System

It's no good having a high performance car if it hasn't got the ability to stop as well as go. So BMW's answer to the problems was simple: fit the same braking system as the M3 Saloon. This uses motor-racing technology with compound disc brakes at the front. These consist of multi-component discs, with the brake-disc friction ring running on a radial anti-friction bearing.

With the conventional, single-piece, grey cast-iron brakes, friction heat generated when applying them is retained in the friction ring and then dissipated slowly to the surrounding components. In extreme cases, however, the thermal load thus created could cause warping or even cracks that could lead to the complete destruction of the offending brake disc.

The M ABS System

The Teves company supplied BMW with its new Mark IV-G ABS system, which had been developed to match the requirements of the new M Roadster. This came complete with a new brake servo to provide optimum response at all times. As on the other Z3 models, the handbrake is a dual servo drum brake acting on the rear wheels via a Bowden cable.

Wheels and Tyres

Manufactured exclusively for the M Roadster (and Coupé), the massive cast-alloy, five-spoke wheels, measuring 7½J × 17 (front) and 9J × 17 (rear), come complete with BMW's special asymmetric 'run-flat' concept. These wheels feature a metal ridge on one side that prevents the tyre coming off the rim if it punctures; so if the worst does happen, the driver of an M Roadster (or Coupé) can drive safely to a convenient stopping point to address the problem.

The massive exhaust silencers of the M version ensured that this was the first BMW in modern times not fitted with a spare wheel, because quite simply, there wasn't

A high performance car needs high performance brakes. The M Roadster (and M Coupé) incorporates compound discs with radial anti-friction bearings, a system allowing the brake discs to expand freely. The result is super-powerful stopping power.

room. Instead, the boot housed a mini-compressor (which works off the cigar lighter) and quick-forming sealant that, according to BMW, 'lasts until the driver is able to reach a service centre'… they both hope! As for the tyres, these are 225/45 ZR-17 (front) and 245/40 ZR-17 (rear) – in other words, more than enough rubber to handle the increased power output.

BMW calls its run-flat tyres the 'M Mobility System'. The official launch Press kit said:

The M Roadster comes with unique 17in wheels (which it shares with the M Coupé), four-pipe exhaust, and roll-over bars as standard.

This decision was taken because punctures are such a rare occurrence today. Statistics show that the average frequency of punctures is only once in every 93,000 miles. So the space and weight saving of this system outweighs the advantage of carrying a spare wheel.

The M Roadster Body: Styling Changes

The M Roadster has the ability to grab attention, and look muscular and capable of reaching 150mph (240km/h) before it has even turned a wheel. All Z3s are attractive, but the M version even more so.

Although it shared the wider rear-wheel arches with the 2.8 (86mm/3.4in), as compared to the 1.8/1.9 four-cylinder models, elsewhere it rapidly left even the 2.8 behind, with its restyled front and rear aprons, a new front air dam and four large-diameter, polished stainless-steel tailpipes. In addition there were large airscoops in the front apron, needed to

Unlike the rest of the Z3 family, the M Roadster did not receive the body styling that was introduced from the 2000 model year. In fact, from this view (except for side grille and wheels) the M looks similar to the pre-2000 2.8.

M Roadster: Standard Equipment (1997)

Air conditioning	Limited slip differential
Additional instruments (oil temp, external temp, clock)	Lockable rear storage box (unless Harmon/Kardon Hi-Fi loudspeaker system fitted)
Alloy wheels: roadster styling	'M' design aerodynamic mirrors
Front: 7.5J × 17in with 225/45 ZR-17	'M' design sports steering wheel with air-bag and leather rim
Rear: 9J × 17in with 245/40 ZR-17	'M' design mobility system
Anti-lock braking system	Moulded soft-top cover
BMW business RDS radio cassette; CD compatible with EON and traffic programme	Passenger air-bag
Central locking with deadlocks	Power steering
Chrome line interior package	Preparation for six-disc autochanger
Deep front spoiler with central air intake	Rear roll-over bars
Electric hood	Remote alarm control
Electrically operated door mirrors	Seat heating
Electrically operated sports seats (manual backrest adjustment)	Service interval indicator
Exterior mirrors painted in body colour	Side-impact protection
Compound disc front brakes (as M3 Evolution)	Side sill panels and wide rear-wheel arches
Four stainless-steel exhaust tailpipes	Tachometer
Free-form twin Halogen headlights	Tool kit
Front electric windows	Transponder immobilizer
Full Nappa leather upholstery	Velour floor mats
Handbrake surround and gear-lever knob in leather	Visible vehicle identification
Height-adjustable passenger seat	Warning triangle and first aid kit
High-level third brake light	White turn signal indicator lenses
Inertia-reel seatbelts with pre-tensioners	Wing-mounted aerial, six speakers
'Lights-on' warning buzzer	

effectively cool the front disc in extreme conditions, in place of the 2.8's fog lamps.

The revised front air dam was to ensure that sufficient air reached the engine to aid efficient cooling, whilst at the same time providing a significant down-force effect to keep the car hugging the road at all times. The tailpipes not only give the Z3M Roadster a unique, aggressive look from the rear, but at the same time they fulfil all noise emission limits required by existing and future envisaged legislation, thanks to their large silencers.

The body had been lowered by an additional 10mm (0.4in), compared to the other Z3 models, allowing not only more cornering ability, but also improving the aerodynamics of the car.

Cosmetic changes included moving the rear number plate to a new home on the boot lid, with the BMW badge moved up behind the brake light, and restyling the side grilles with horizontal chrome fins, white indicator lenses and the all-important M logo. Then the mirrors, both inside and outside, are much rounder in profile than the squarer items specified for other Z3s. And finally there is the colour-keyed roof, several of the paint options being exclusive to the M version.

In the Cockpit

To justify what was an enormous leap in cost as compared to the 2.8/3.0 models, BMW not only did as much as possible externally to

The side grilles are special to the M Series Z3 models (the Roadster and Coupé).

The famous M (Motorsport) logo.

distance the M Roadster from its lesser brothers, it also gave considerable attention to the interior of the car, and in particular the cockpit area.

To start with there were, as standard fitment, contrasting coloured leather panels on the seats, doors, steering-wheel insert and dashboard. Three new circular dials adorned the centre console, along with chrome hi-lights on

the gear gate and ventilation controls; the tachometer also sported an 'M Roadster' logo.

On the rest of the Z3 Roadster range, roll-over bars were a cost-option extra; but on the Z3M these come as standard, being fitted behind both the driver and the passenger headrests.

As with the other Z3s, security from unwanted attention was seen by BMW as

M Roadster: Interior and Exterior Colours (1977)	
Metallic paint	Boston Green
	Cosmos Black
	Arctic Silver
	Estoril Blue ★
Non-metallic paint	Alpine White
	Evergreen ★
	Imola Red ★
	Dakar Yellow ★
Full nappa leather	Black/black
	Dark grey/black
	Estoril blue/black
	Imola red/black
	Kyalami orange/black
Hood colours	Black
	Classic red ★
	Dark blue ★
★ These colours are not available for the 1.8, 1.9 and 2.8 models.	

M Roadster interior, featuring sports seats (two-tone leather) 'M' steering wheel, chrome gearchange box surround, and six chrome surrounds in the central console. Although the seats are fully adjustable, the steering wheel, like the rest of the Z3 family, is not.

Like the rest of the Z3 Series, the M Roadster's cockpit is a comfortable place to be. Besides the M logo on the steering wheel, there is also one on the tachometer.

Chrome surrounds for heater/ventilation controls, oil temperature, water temperature and clock.

exceedingly important. All models therefore, including the Z3M, feature the EWS II rolling code immobilizer. This electronic device is fully automatic, and operates independently of the central locking and remote control. It is described in more detail in Chapter 5.

Summary

In creating the M version, BMW built what many consider to be the ultimate roadster – or at least one at something like an affordable price. The well-respected motoring journalist Peter Robinson wrote about the Z3M roadster in *Autocar* during 1998, and had this to say:

> The M Roadster is in a different league from the sports car arena, where the Z3 competes. This car aims higher. Much higher. With 321bhp in an engine bay that has always cried out for more, the M Roadster has left the world of Porsche Boxsters and Merc SLKs and, with a glimpse over its shoulder at the legendary AC Cobra for inspiration, has gone chasing the Porsche 911 RS and TVR Griffith.

Top Gear magazine had this to say of the M Roadster:

> There's a car that arguably comes close to winning best driver's car, never mind best roadster – BMW's

M Roadster with AC Schnitzer package, including exhaust, modified rear spoiler, wider wheels and chrome roll-over bars.

mighty, Z3-based M Roadster. Rally champion Mark Higgins declared the M Roadster more fun to drive than either an EVO VI or a Ferrari 360 when we did a rear-wheel-drive versus four-wheel-drive TV item recently!

But, as with everything, there are others who don't agree, typical comments including 'Hugely fast and better looking than its lesser Z3 brother, but it is still strangely uninvolving for a sports car.'

But love it or hate it, the truth is, you simply cannot ignore the M Roadster. Not only does it look great, but it combines a rawness and sense of purpose, together with a level of sophistication unmatched for its purchase price in the roadster market.

The latest E46 M3 (a 2002 model is shown) uses the same engine and exhaust as the Z3M.

Road-Testing the M Roadster

Now, with the arrival of the even more powerful V8-engined Z8, the M Roadster is no longer the fastest accelerating BMW car. However, that doesn't stop it being an awesome, high-performance speed machine. Having previously driven an M3 Saloon, I was as least reasonably familiar with the engine. But it is worth saying that the 3.2 litre motor is not only indecently quick (321bhp), but also fantastically tractable – so flexible, in fact, that it will still surge forwards at less than 2,000rpm in top (fifth). Of course, the M Roadster doesn't inherit the six-speed gearbox of the saloon. But in all honesty, with such a tractable power unit, who really cares – and it's one less gear to keep changing every time you use the box.

The five-speed gearbox has synchromesh on all ratios, and is shared with the 2.8/3.0 Z3s. To be honest, the change quality is not as good as the four-cylinder models or the 2.0/2.2 sixes, the M's box needing the driver to select the gear, rather than just simply doing it. The clutch action, like the other Z Series cars, is perfectly weighed and reasonably light.

By nailing the throttle and taking the engine up to near peak revs, it's easy to smash the 0–62mph barrier in just over 5sec. Even without any form of traction control, except a 25 per cent lock-up limited slip diff, the M Roadster does not let go easily. Only when giving the car a big boot full in first or second gear out of a junction, will it attempt to do anything scary – and even then, its progressive style can be caught before things get out of hand. Perhaps this, and its incredible ability to glue itself to the road and not 'unstick', is partly responsible for some journalists to have labelled the M Roadster 'uninvolving'.

Although supremely flexible, the M engine is a rev-happy device, maximum rpm being 7,400. This truly is an engine to kill for. I was able to make a direct comparison between the M Roadster and a 5-litre TVR Chimaera. The British car I found was much more of a handful when pushing hard. The TVR had not only less grip, but was also harder to control – notably in the wet. Only on the straights could the Chimaera's extra cubes attempt to make up what it lost on the twisty bits.

Also, compared to the TVR's all-singing and all-dancing crescendo of noise, the BMW is almost a restful place to be; relaxing almost. The M Roadster also stops more quickly thanks to its superb compound split-hub, ventilated, cross-dialled racing discs with ABS. In comparison, the TVR's brakes work, and that's all.

Besides having five instead of six speeds, the M Roadster's other minus point compared to the latest M3 Saloon is the fact of its not having the Z axle. Instead it has the conventional set-up from the lesser-engined Z3s, but with re-engineering to stiffen the whole assembly. Even so, it doesn't really compromise the handling too much. The chassis is set up to understeer. But if, halfway through a bend, you either lift your foot off the throttle or bury it, the M Roadster rear slides round, but nice and gently, giving you plenty of time to balance the throttle, apply some opposite lock and continue 'back on the rails'.

'Back on the rails' is what the M Roadster is really about: drive it sensibly, and you simply can't go wrong, the car feeling as if it is on rails as you negotiate the bends. There's just a hint of body structure wobble and shimmy on less than perfect road surfaces, but some of this is due to the wide and grippy tyres increasing the suspension settings. But otherwise, the steering can only be described as meaty and accurate.

The M's cabin is like all Z3s, ergonomically correct, but the top-of-the-range model also manages to exude a de luxe feel, too. It not only works, but looks great as well, with its sculpted two-tone leather, additional chrome and dials, plus of course the 'M' logo on tacho, steering wheel and doorwell kick bars. And it comes with all the goodies (well, almost) including air con, roll-over bars and electric roof as a standard fitment.

Would I want one? Yes please!

8   The Coupé

Amazingly the Coupé was born from an idea hatched by a group of BMW workers in their spare time during an after-hours get-together. The result is one of the most distinctive cars of recent times.

Unlike the Z3 and Z3M Roadster models, the coupé version was never part of the original scheme of things, but a car born out of a chance meeting after work in the underground garage of BMW's R&D centre in Munich. At this get-together was a five-man team of engineers. They realized that attempting to have an entirely new car was out of the question; it would simply have been too expensive for the number of sales it was likely to generate.

The meeting came at a time when the early Z3 Roadster prototypes (which included the M version) had reached the full-size stage. This then led to the assembled engineers quickly realizing that within the Z3 design there was the potential for a genuine GT car. They also appreciated that having a stiffer body shell would improve both rigidity and refinement; furthermore, it would provide more responsive handling.

Whether you like it or not, you can't ignore BMW's 'breadvan'. Actually, although labelled the 'Coupé', it's more akin to a high performance estate such as the Reliant Scimitar or Volvo ES 1800.

Basically the Coupé project revolved around using the Z3 front half, chassis and drive train (the 2.8 and 3.2, not the four-cylinder engines), with an integral steel roof and new tail section.

Creating the Original Mock-Up

At first the engineers didn't bother too much with the restyling exercise that would ultimately be needed, but set about creating the engineering package. This meant removing the rear wings and boot lid of the roadster, and as they began to cover the exposed rear end with components such as roof bars, foam plastic, wood and surface foil, a solitary styling man was brought into their confidence.

Of course, all this was still very much a secret; certainly senior BMW management knew nothing of the exercise. As one of the team was later to recall: 'It was like building a car in days gone by.' There was little or no use of modern information technology, which meant no full-size computerized sketches, no detailed drafting drawings, just a small team of like-minded individuals hand-crafting a new car in their own spare time, and almost totally outside BMW's normal highly controlled development process.

Only when the wood and clay full-size mock-up was actually completed did the friends

find the confidence to show their creation to BMW's product chief, Dr Wolfgang Reitzle.

The Arguments Begin

Dr Reitzle had not got to the position he held without a very good grasp of what would, and what would not work in the automobile world. And he was quick to realize that here was not only a viable idea that could be put into production relatively cheaply, but also one that would

From the cockpit forward, the Z3M Coupé is very much like its M Roadster brother, only Coupé logos on the kickplate and tachometer make things different.

Compare these two pictures to appreciate the crucial differences between the Z3M Coupé...and the Z3 2.8 (later superseded by the 3.0) sold in some countries like Germany, but not Britain: side grilles; wheels; exhaust; front and rear spoilers; and rear number plate location.

give the Z3 series more depth, and attract a new type of customer. Reitzle also realized that: 'This car is not built to be everyone's darling.'

This was going to cause controversy not only amongst BMW employees, but in the press and general public, too. BMW's special projects chief, Dipl. Ing. Burkhard Goeschel (and the man behind the Z3), summed up the coupé as follows: 'Some people saw it and were thrilled. Others were, let's say, more reserved' – which actually meant they didn't like the shape. He went on to reveal: 'There was a long debate on the car, with extreme opinions, and there was nothing in between. If you didn't love it at first sight, you hated it. In the end we decided that what we call "emancipated navigators" would buy it.'

The Design is Finalized

On the questions of practicality and costs, there was never any suggestion of lengthening the wheelbase to make it a full four-seater, or even a two-plus-two, because it was only by utilizing the Z3 floorplan that the Coupé project would be viable.

Although BMW themselves viewed the Coupé as a modern incarnation of cars such as the Triumph GT6 or MGB GT, in reality the idea of extending the roofline all the way back, as on an estate, made the finished article far more akin to the Reliant Scimitar GTE or Volvo ES1800. As *Autocar* commented: 'The coupé breaks every styling principle', and went on to say: 'The Coupé M is brutal, not elegant; exciting, not bland. No way does it look as if it was designed from a clean sheet of paper; more that it evolved like a Californian custom car'.

And that is exactly what BMW's Coupé is all about: in a world filled with computerized blandness and political correctness, the proportions of the BMW 'breadvan' are dramatically opposed to the utterly alien, tidy but boring packaging of most of today's automobiles. In fact in the author's opinion, Dr Wolfgang Reitzle, BMW, and most of all those five brave engineers struck a blow for the unique car lobby when creating and authorizing the coupé for production. And it proves that occasionally it is still possible to do something differently.

Aimed at Individualists

Jurgan Pawlik, in charge of product management of BMW M Sport, said at the launch of the M Coupé in 1997: 'We see the buyers as real individualists who love the unusual styling. I don't think any buyers will ask if the neighbours like the car.'

Unlike the Z3 Roadster series, the relatively small rear section − tail, if you will − is at odds with its aggressively long snout. But the Coupé is far more balanced in this respect, with aggressiveness at both ends − though of course this has led most observers to refer to the design as 'brutal' or even 'madcap'.

These two views illustrate the long nose area of the Z3 Series, including the Z3M Coupé, its lines are probably the most aggressive of the entire Z3 clan. No wonder some members of the press corps have referred to the Coupé as 'brutal'.

Sixes Only

Originally, when the Coupé project was first given the go-ahead by Dr Reitzle, the Munich company considered the possibility of offering it in the same engine sizes as the Z3, at that time 1.8, 1.9, 2.8 and 3.2. But this was soon rejected, as it was generally agreed that the four-cylinder engines didn't provide enough 'oomph' to match the aggressive line of the coupé. The car has therefore only been offered with six-cylinder units. Only the M Coupé, with its full-power 320bhp 3.2 engine, has ever been imported by the Bracknell-based BMW

AC Schnitzer-modified, German-registered Z3 Coupé 2.8: the front spoiler with 'flippers', and Series III 18in alloy wheels.

The Z3M Coupé (1998)	
Engine	Liquid-cooled, twenty-four valve, dohc, inline, six-cylinder, with double VANOS and Digital Motor Electronics (DME)
Displacement	3,201cc
Bore	91mm
Stroke	86.4mm
Compression ratio	11.3:1
Transmission	Five-speed, manual, all-synchromesh gearbox
Doors	Two
Seats	Two
Chassis	n/a
Bodywork	Steel, galvanized, with bolt-on panels
Drive	Rear wheel
Wheels	Front 7.5J × 17 in
	Rear 9J × 17 in
Tyres	Front 225/45 ZR-17 flat-run type
	Rear 245/40 ZR-17 flat-run type
Dimensions	
Overall length	4,025mm (158.5in)
Overall width	1,740mm (68.5in)
Overall height	1,280mm (50in)
Wheelbase	2,459mm (97in)
Dry weight	1,465kg (3,230lb)
Max power	321bhp @ 7,400rpm
Max torque	258lb ft (350Nm) @ 3,250rpm
Top speed	155mph (250km/h), limited
0–62mph	5.3sec
(European model specifications quoted)	

TOP: *The first of BMW's Z Series family, the Z1, arrived in 1988 and used the 2,494cc six-cylinder engine from the 325 3 Series saloon.*

MIDDLE: *Capable of reaching 60mph (100km/h) in less than 8sec, the Z1 had a maximum speed of 136mph (220km/h).*

BOTTOM: *Built at the new Spartanburg plant in South Carolina, the first Z3s – the 1.8 and 1.9 (the latter is seen here) – used four-cylinder engines; they made their debut in early 1996.*

Four-pot engines, like those found in the 3 Series saloon, offered a reasonable mix of performance and economy, at an affordable price. This is the eight-valve 1.9 unit from the confusingly badged '1.8' sold on the British market from the 2000 model year.

BELOW: The Z3 2.8 arrived in 1997. It was virtually a new car, with a much more powerful six-cylinder engine, as well as a wider track, larger/wider tyres, revised suspension, revised body, traction control, limited slip differential, a stonger gearbox and more powerful brakes. This car has optional hardtop and chrome trim, including the 16in Z-star wheels.

When BMW revealed the prototype of the 3.2-litre Z3M Roadster at the 1996 Geneva Show, it not only completed its new Roadster family, but the M Roadster was also its fastest-accelerating production car yet.

Displacing 3,201cc, the M3-derived engine developed a whopping 321bhp (Americans got 'only' 240bhp).

For those wanting more room – if not more seats – BMW offered the M Coupé. Amazingly, this was never planned, but 'happened' following a chance discussion by a group of workers after hours!

The front section of the Coupé is identical to its Roadster brother, but the stiffer bodyshell allows greater extremes when cornering.

There's no getting away from the fact that the M Coupé looks a mean, aggressive speed machine, from any angle.

ABOVE: A revised Z3 Series (except for the M variants) arrived for the 2000 model year. As well as a new 2-litre (replaced by a 2.2 unit from 2001) six, the rear body was restyled, together with the interior and the choice of new-style wheels. But it was very much a cosmetic exercise, rather than a dynamic one.

RIGHT: A 2000 Z3 2.8 with speedster humps.

BELOW: The interior of a 2000 series Z3, showing the new central console, steering wheel and revised (leather) seats. This car has the blue leather option for the console and dash.

A 2001 Z3 2.2 six-cylinder Sports model. The 'Sports' prefix didn't mean extra performance, instead there were features such as 17in alloy wheels, aluminium-effect central console, sports seats – and more!

From the 2000 model year, double VANOS valve gear, instead of single VANOS, was used in the 2.8 and 2.0 six-cylinder engines. 2.2 and 3.0 litre (still with double VANOS) arrived for 2001.

A 2001 Z3 2.2 out on test in the Scottish Highlands in the summer of that year. The new 2,171cc engine produced 170bhp and was a considerable improvement over the outgoing 2.0 unit which it replaced.

ABOVE: The Z07 Coupé, together with the very similar Roadster concept car, was the forerunner of the Z8. The Z07 cars were only produced in prototype guise, and made their debut at the Tokyo Motor Show towards the end of 1997.

RIGHT: The Z8 made its public debut at the Frankfurt Show in September 1999. Clearly based on the Z07 concept car, the Z8 was the work of the young Danish designer, Henrik Fisker.

LEFT: *Like the Z3, the Z8 was very much a retro design, and in the latter case was also a modern 507, but with the very latest technology. For power it used a 4,941cc, thirty-two-valve, V8 engine producing 400bhp at 6,600rpm.*

BELOW: *The X Coupé of 2001 was a concept car with some radical styling cues; like the Z3's replacement, the Z4, it was the work of BMW's design chief, the American Chris Bangle.*

The Chris Bangle-designed Z4 made its debut in the summer of 2002. Initially it was powered by 2.5- and 3.0-litre six-cylinder engines. The styling is controversial, to say the least.

Another Schnitzer-modified Coupé, this time an M version, with the company's wheels, rear spoiler and exhaust.

BELOW: Out on the open road the M Coupé is an aggressive performer, thanks to its stiffer body shell, and better handling and roadholding when compared to the Roadster.

GB organization; the USA got the detuned 240bhp 3.2 M motor. The domestic German market customers, on the other hand, have had the choice of both the 2.8 (later replaced by the 3.0) and the 320bhp 3.2 M power unit. It is highly unlikely that a Coupé version of the new Z4 will be built.

Body Rigidity

Despite having a wider track for the six-cylinder models, BMW was unable to entirely get rid of scuttle shake on its Z3 Roadster range, even on the higher performance cars – which were meant to resolve the accusation of lack of performance normally pointed at the 1.8 and

Tail-end view of the M Coupé. There are several differences compared to the M Roadster, including rear lights, boot release, rear wiper, and lots more. The four tailpipes are shared with the Roadster.

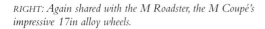

Enormous air scoops are needed on the front spoiler on the M Coupé (and the M Roadster) to assist the cooling of the massive ventilated front disc brakes.

RIGHT: Again shared with the M Roadster, the M Coupé's impressive 17in alloy wheels.

1.9 models. However, bump deflection was impossible to avoid on poor road surfaces.

With more than double the body rigidity over the roadster, the coupé's stiffer structure meant the virtual elimination of bump steer; it also meant much superior refinement and improved driver feedback, and thus a greater responsiveness. As one journalist put it: '... it converts the Z3M from a mere point-and-squirt Roadster, at its best for an hour on a Sunday morning, to a serious GT car.'

It's worth noting that the Z3M Coupé weighs 110kg (243lb) more than its roadster brother.

A Major Flaw

Both the Z3M Roadster and the Coupé, at least in its M guise, have one serious flaw: they retain the tiny 51ltr (11gal) fuel tank. This can be justified for the 1.9 and 1.8 four-cylinder models, it is just about acceptable on the 2.8/3.0 sixes – but it is totally inadequate on the 3.2 M Series engines. The development team did take a serious look at increasing the tank capacity, but they soon realized that because it would involve changing the Z3 floorplan, it would prove horrendously expensive to justify when production volumes were never likely to be high.

Boot Space

Whilst it was obliged to retain the small Roadster tank, the Coupé was at least able to do something about boot space. In contrast to the Roadster's 165ltr (5.7cu ft), the Coupé's capacity was a much greater 210ltr (7.4cu ft) – and an impressive 410ltr (14.5cu ft) if one loaded the boot up to the roof and employed the safety net.

And while on the subject of space, the Coupé remained strictly for two, as there's not even an emergency seat in the rear. But at least this is honest, by comparison with the rear 'passenger' space in, say, an Alfa GTV or a Jaguar XKR.

The Coupé is also a better bet for those wanting to go camping or touring, thanks to a significant increase in carrying space.

Heart of the Matter

Away from the styling and increased rigidity, the Coupé's other main attraction is its engine. All BMW sixes on offer are noted for their silken smoothness – even the full power 3.2 M – and flexibility, and also for their high level of reliability. And there are no cam-belt changes to worry over, as the cams are driven by chains. Another plus-point is the excellent fuel economy, particularly in the 2.8/3.0 units.

Close-up of the M Coupé rear light and 'M' badge.

Mirrors are another item not found on the non-M Z cars. They are much rounder in profile and thus more streamlined.

Further Advantages

There are yet more advantages of taking the Coupé route: high-speed cruising is much easier, wind noise is suppressed, the engine note is quieter and stability is superior – plus that much bigger luggage-carrying ability. So the Coupé has its own following. Of course, you can't put down the hood on a sunny day, and maybe, to some, the styling isn't as attractive as the emotive

In this view the M Coupé almost resembles a hot hatch, rather than an exotic supercar. Top Gear magazine voted it 'Driver's Car of the Year' in 2000.

M Coupé instruments. Tachometer has 'M Coupé' inscription.

roadster. But even the press has come round to liking the idea, with *Top Gear* magazine voting the M coupé their 'Driver's Car Winner' in the year 2000. Here are a few of their comments, made when presenting the award:

Reach a nice clear alpine road, and you'll soon be punching the throttle and kicking out the rear with a grin from ear to ear.

The Coupé gives motorway running that's quiet and effortless, and the ride quality will allow a passenger to snooze as you cruise.

Sitting in that driver-orientated cockpit, one could be in an RAF fighter plane.

With only about 250 coming into the country each year there's also an element of exclusivity, and in years to come, it's bound to become a classic.

With a silky smooth, 321-horsepower straight-six mounted up front, rear-wheel drive, a limited-slip differential and no traction control: it has all the right ingredients for the ultimate in driver-controlled fun.

With those stylish, idiosyncratic looks and rear wheel-directed, adrenalin-rousing power, this Beemer is the ultimate boy racer's machine. It had to be the No. 1 driver's car.

With this endorsement, the BMW Coupé can be considered as one of the truly great sports cars of modern times. And outside the UK, potential customers had the chance to buy not only the 3.2 M-engined coupé, but also the cheaper 2.8 or, from 2000, the 3.0-engined car. The latter is probably the best of the breed, being around 25–30 per cent less expensive to buy, and in terms of performance almost as quick. And as an added bonus, the 231bhp, 2,979cc engine is much more suited to the more rigid-bodied Coupé format than the open roadster version. What a pity, therefore, that British enthusiasts were denied such an excellent car.

9 Specialists

More than any other BMW model, the Z3 Series seems to act as a magnet to the aftermarket brigade, with the warehouses full of bolt-on goodies, and tuning shops selling extra performance. Even BMW realized this, and offered a vast array of factory options, either as original factory-fitted components, or dealer-fit parts. Then there are the 'factory-approved' specialist suppliers, Alpina and AC Schnitzer. The advantage of going for these two names is the same as the full-factory items, in that your car's warranty is not affected provided they are fitted by your friendly local BMW dealer. Fit non-approved items, however, and if something goes wrong, BMW will help you.

Besides the huge number of European specialists, there is also a strong hardcore of American-based firms specializing in the Z3.

AC Schnitzer

Based in Aachen, AC Schnitzer is a division of the Kohl Automotive group; it is also the most widely known name in the BMW tuning and accessories business. Schnitzer offers a vast range of services; they even build complete cars, using BMW models as a basis, including the Z3.

AC Schnitzer logo.

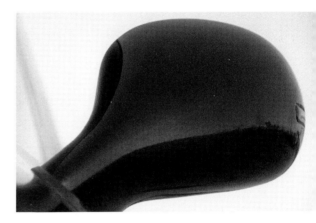

AC Schnitzer M-type mirror. This can be fitted to all Z Series cars.

Besides major components such as wheels, body kits, racing suspension kits, sports exhausts (often in stainless steel), interiors, and its famous 'Short Shift' gearchange conversion, the company offers many smaller, less expensive items, right down to an AC Schnitzer adhesive badge, retailing for just over £6. A particularly neat accessory for the Z3 range is the aluminium pedal set and driver's footrest.

On the race circuit, AC Schnitzer and BMW have enjoyed a winning combination for over three decades, with drivers such as Gerhard Berger and Jacques Lafitte benefiting from Schnitzer components.

From the author's experience, the Short Shift gearchange conversion, whilst suiting the lesser-powered models (the 1.8, 1.9 and 2.0 six), does not work so well with the stronger gearbox as

The Schnitzer V8

Based at Aachen, the Schnitzer company has had a long association with BMW, and together with Alpina offers not only accessories and tuning equipment for the Z3 range, but also builds a very special V8 version. Whilst BMW chose the M3 V6 engine for its Roadster, Schnitzer shoehorned a V8 from the 540i into the Z3. Incredibly, this voluminous 4,398cc (92 × 82.7mm) powerplant has been slotted under the bonnet of the Z3 without major surgery.

Unlike the M Roadster, the Schnitzer V8 is not intended as an out-and-out sports car; instead, it is more in the cruiser mould of the 2.8/3.0 BMW Z3s, the V8 engine from the 540i saloon being considered by the Schnitzer team as 'better suited to versatile roadster performance than the six-cylinder inline from the BMW M3'. Schnitzer could also have added that the V8 lets out a fabulous 'lion roar' when running at high speeds, but has the added advantage of total docility when opening lower down the rev range.

Already offering more than enough grunt, Schnitzer increased its maximum torque to a super-impressive 440Nm (at 4,300rpm). This, together with a maximum power output of 310bhp at 5,800rpm, gives the Z3 V8 the performance of the M Roadster, with the advantage of being superior at lower speeds.

So a quiet day's cruising out in the country or a track day are equally breathtaking. At moderate speed on country back roads, with the hood down, the engine is almost silent – below 2,000rpm it is inaudible over the road noise. But turn up the wick and let the thunder begin!

The biggest surprise, though, is that the Schnitzer V8 is hardly any heavier than a standard Z3, the V8 engine actually being lighter than the M3 unit. But the Schnitzer is heavier at 1,520kg (3,352lb), some 10kg (22lb) more than the M3 Roadster.

The biggest drawback of the V8 is its fuel consumption, which is around 18mpg (16ltr/100km). To offset this, the Schnitzer V8's boot contains a 40ltr (8.8gal) supplementary fuel tank.

As for performance, Schnitzer quotes a top speed of 160mph (257km/h), and a 0–62mph (0–100km/h) acceleration figure of 5.2sec.

The cockpit of the Schnitzer Roadster is very similar to the M Roadster, but with the seats, central console and dashboard re-upholstered in buffalo leather.

But it is the character of the V8 engine that really turns the Schnitzer Z3 into pure supercar material.

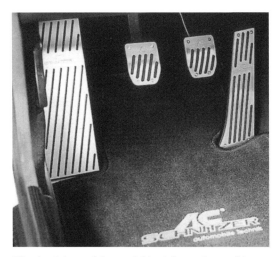

The aluminium pedal set and driver's footrest is one of the most popular AC Schnitzer items; it looks good, too.

Schnitzer's famous 'short-shift' gearchange conversion: it gives a closer change. This works best on the lesser models (1.8, 1.9, 2.0 and 2.2 Z3).

103

A selection of AC Schnitzer alloy wheels. Top left to right: Type II, Type II racing, Type III with open spokes and bolted-up rim. Bottom: Type III, with and without inserts.

fitted to the 2.8, 3.0 and M models. In these, the gearchange (upwards) is already quite stiff, and fitting the Schnitzer conversion does not improve things. On the smaller-engined cars it is delightful to use, closing up the gearchange action.

Probably the most popular of the more expensive components are the various wheels. Available in 17in and 18in sizes in a variety of designs, some of these require 7mm (front) and 10mm (rear) spacers.

Alpina

Alpina has been associated with BMW since 1963, and is based in the small town of Büchloe in the eastern Allgau region of Bavaria. The company builds around 500 vehicles (all BMW-based) a year, plus a range of accessories and body kits for various BMWs, including the Z3 Series.

Alpina has been associated with BMW since 1963; it is based in the small town of Büchloe in the eastern region of Bavaria.

The famous twenty-spoke Alpina wheels, normally found on upmarket 5 or 7 Series saloons; these can also be supplied for the Z3, together with a number of other components including gear knobs, steering wheels and suspension springs.

Alpina's distinctive twenty-spoke aluminium wheels are a company hallmark, featuring a lockable, light alloy hub cover. Other components include body kits, steering wheels, gear-lever knobs and floor carpets.

Hartge

Hartge is another famous name specializing in high performance BMWs and aftermarket goodies and tuning equipment. For example, Hartge (the British importers Autobahn Ltd, based in East Harling, Norfolk), like AC Schnitzer, offers a V8 version of BMW's M3 Roadster. This beautifully styled car (with Hartge 18in wheels), unique paintwork and individually crafted interior, is marketed in small numbers as the Hartge Z3 M Roadster 5.0 V8. The company claims a top speed of 169mph (272km/h), and 0–62mph (0–100km/h) in a breathtaking 4.8sec. Maximum torque is quoted as 510Nm at 3,550rpm.

It is worth mentioning that Hartge also offers the 5.0 V8 engine in 3, 5, and 7 Series saloon guise.

Hartge is another famous name specializing in high performance goodies for BMW, including the Z Series cars. This is a 2001 advertisement from the British importers, the Norfolk-based Autobahn concern.

10   Z3 Update

During the late summer of 1999 BMW brought out an updated Z3 range, excluding the M Roadster and M Coupé. At the time, this was referred to by many observers as a 'makeover' (*Autocar*, September 1999).

Highlights at a Glance

- New 2.0 model with 150bhp six-cylinder engine;
- New entry level 1.8 (1.9-litre);
- Chrome rings around headlamps;

- Z3 became the widest model range in the roadster market;
- Wider, more curvy rear bodywork;
- Double VANOS variable valve timing for 2.0 and 2.8 models;
- Steptronic auto gearbox;
- Dynamic Stability Control (DSC III) now available as an option;
- New interior colours and materials;
- Improved sound-proofing for soft-top roof;
- New centre console and switchgear;
- Five new exterior colours.

During the late summer of 1999, BMW introduced an updated Z3 range for the 2000 model year. This comprised a revised 2.8 with double VANOS (shown with optional speedster covers and 17in alloy wheels), and a new 2.0 six and 8-valve 1,895cc, four coded '1.8'.

Introduction to the UK

By 1999, one in five of all roadsters sold in the UK was a Z3, with British sales of the various Z3s during 1998 reaching a total of 5,282. This made it comfortably the third best-seller in an increasingly competitive market, behind the MGF and Mazda MX-5 (both having a considerably lower purchase-price structure).

BMW GB managing director Kevin Gaskell commented:

> Since 1995, when the first left-hand-drive models went on sale, over 170,000 Z3s (worldwide) have been sold. In less than three years of sales in the UK we have sold almost 13,000. With the latest revisions to the model, I am convinced that we can strengthen our position further, despite strong competition.

Driver Survey

BMW realized that its customers were the best people to speak to when making an update to its model range. And it also realized that the Z3 buyer was different to buyers of its other models. What it found was not only did they tend to be younger (except a group of older owners), but they were more likely to be single; just 13 per cent had children in the household. One in seven buyers of a Z3 also owned a motorcycle, whilst almost one in three owned another BMW car.

They also found that one in three owners was female, compared to an average of one in five across the whole BMW range; and 75 per cent of Z3s were purchased privately rather than by a company.

The new base model from the 2000 model year (introduced in mid-1999) was the '1.8'. This featured the 118bhp eight-valve four-cylinder engine from the E46 3 Series saloon. And in the UK it retailed for less than £20,000 (£19,995). This car has an optional chrome windscreen surround and door handles, plus alloy wheels.

In a survey of customers buying a Z3 when it first went on sale, a staggering 90 per cent said that their primary reason for purchase was either style or image. The full results were:

Style, 67 per cent
Price, 25 per cent
Image, 23 per cent
Sports car, 12 per cent
Reliability, 12 per cent
Exclusivity, 12 per cent

Entry Model: The New 1.8

Of the revised range, the entry model for the UK was the new 1.8. Actually this definition was misleading, as the actual engine size was

The 1,895cc (85 × 83.5mm), dohc, eight-valve engine is a smooth performer thanks to its twin-balancer shafts. Although on paper producing 'only' 118bhp, its excellent low-down torque makes it a creditable performer, and not quite the Cinderella everyone had expected.

The Z3 1.8 Roadster (2000)	
Engine	Liquid-cooled, eight-valve, dohc inline, four-cylinder
Displacement	1,895cc
Bore	85mm
Stroke	83.5mm
Compression ratio	9.7:1
Transmission	Five-speed, manual
Doors	Two
Seats	Two
Chassis	Unitary construction
Bodywork	Steel, galvanized, with bolt-on panels
Suspension	Front: spring-strut front axle with anti-dive and anti-roll bar
	Rear: semi-trailing arm rear axle, anti-squat and anti-dive; anti-roll bar
Drive	Rear wheel
Wheels	Steel 7J × 16 front and rear
Tyres	225/50 R16 92 front and rear
Dimensions	
Overall length	4,050mm (159in)
Overall width	1,858mm (73in)
Overall height	1,293mm (51in)
Wheelbase	2,446mm (96.3in)
Dry weight	1,295kg (2,855lb)
Max power	118bhp @ 5,500rpm
Max torque	133lb ft (180Nm) @ 3,900pm
Top speed	122mph (196km/h)
0–62mph	9.7sec

1,895cc (85 × 83.5mm). There had of course been a '1.8' Z3 right from the start, but this had never been sold in the UK, and in any case was a real 1.8 with an engine size of 1,796cc. With a price tag of less than £20,000 (£19,995 on-the-road April 2000), the new '1.8' competed against the like of the Mazda MX-5, the MGF and the Toyota MR2.

The original 140bhp, sixteen-valve, M44-engined, Z3 four-cylinder model had been axed for failing to meet forthcoming emissions targets. This had led to the BMW Z3 development team utilizing the eight-valver from the latest E46 3 Series saloon and coupé models.

Torque, Not Power

On paper, the eight-valve engine put out 118bhp, as against 140bhp from the outgoing four-cylinder model. However, this only told

part of the story, because although the eight-valve powerplant might not have the horses, it more than made up for that by delivering excellent torque. This was particularly evident lower down the scale. Where the old sixteen-valver needed revving to exploit its performance, the new engine delivered a solid push right from the off – certainly enough to provide fun both in an urban and a country lane environment. Only above 5,000rpm did BMW's base Z3 get a little breathless. And let's face it, it's the sub-5,000 range that most drivers use most of the time. And not only this, but thanks to twin balancer shafts, the latest eight-valve engine was particularly smooth.

Studying the power curve compared with the discarded sixteen-valver makes for interesting reading. The torque curve sees the eight-valve-engined car ahead, all the way up

The new four-cylinder Z3 was fitted with the 1,895cc, 118bhp, eight-valve engine from the then current 3 Series.

to 4,000rpm. In fact, not just this, but the eight-valve four managed to stay with the new 2.0-litre six-cylinder Z3 as well! OK, the eight-valve engine runs out of puff, just when the others come alive, but to assist this, BMW engineers had endowed the '1.8' with taller gearing. The four also weighed some 50kg (110lb) less than the 2.0 six. With a 0–62mph (0–100km/h) figure of 9.7sec, and a maximum speed of 122mph (196km/h), the '1.8' won't set the world on fire. But if you consider that the classic Austin Healey 3000 originally struggled to break the 11sec barrier, owners can feel quite proud of themselves: not only are they driving a car that looks far more expensive than it actually cost them to buy, they will also be saving at the pumps, with an excellent overall fuel consumption of 36.2mpg (7.8ltr/100km). And of course by removing the '1.8' chrome badge at the rear, the uninformed observer won't have a clue as to what the size of your engine is in any case!

When testing a 2001 model '1.8', the author was much more impressed than he expected. Compared to the car it effectively replaced, the newcomer was punchier in the low–mid range, smoother, better equipped and cheaper. What more could you want? Of course, it doesn't have the outright performance of the 2.8/3.0 sixes or the M version, but all these are considerably more expensive in terms of initial cost and running expenses, such as servicing, fuel and insurance.

Z3 1.8 Standard Equipment (2000 Model Year)
- Driver and passenger airbags;
- Pyrotechnic seat-belt latch tensioners;
- Side-impact door beams;
- Remote-control central locking with alarm and immobilizer;
- Anti-lock brakes;
- Automatic stability control and traction;
- Steel 16in wheels with 225/50VR sixteen tyres;

A new 2.0 six (with the 150bhp engine from the 520i) made its debut. This view shows off the revised rear-end styling, with fluted rear wings and other changes.

ABOVE: The new 2.0 six effectively replaced the superseded 1.9 140bhp four in BMW's Z3 range. Although performance wasn't greatly different, the engine was smoother and had better torque figures.

LEFT: Interior of the 2000 Z3 2.0; note the optional roll-over bars.

BELOW: The new 2.0 with the roof up. This car has the optional chrome side grilles, but is otherwise standard. Note the new-style alloy wheels.

Four engine under-bonnet views of the 2.0 litre six-cylinder Z3. As on the 2.8,...

...the battery is located in the boot. Side view: note the front suspension mounting in the foreground with the 'BMW'-inscribed cam cover behind it.

The front view shows how full the engine bay is with the six-cylinder engine...

...and the nearside view, showing fuel injectors, oil dipstick, and the air filtration box.

- All-round disc brakes;
- Electronically operated, body-coloured door mirrors;
- Rear-view mirror with automatic anti-dazzle function;

- Partial electronic adjustment of driver's seat (for height and leg-room);
- Electronic windows;
- BMW business RDS radio/cassette with preparation for CD autochanger.

The Z3 2.0 Roadster (2000)

Engine	Liquid-cooled, twenty-four-valve, dohc, inline, six-cylinder with single VANOS
Displacement	1,991cc
Bore	80mm
Stroke	66mm
Compression ratio	11:1
Transmission	Five-speed, manual, five-speed Steptronic automatic ★
Doors	Two
Seats	Two
Chassis	Unitary construction
Bodywork	Steel, galvanized, with bolted-on panels
Suspension	Front: spring-strut front axle with anti-dive and anti-roll bar
	Rear: semi-trailing arm rear axle, anti-squat and anti-dive; anti-roll bar.
Drive	Rear wheel
Wheels	Cast alloy 7J × 16 front and rear
Tyres	225/50 R16 92V front and rear

Dimensions

Overall length	4,050mm (159in)
Overall width	1,858mm (73in)
Overall height	1,293mm (51in)
Wheelbase	2,459mm (96.8in)
Dry weight	1,345kg (2,966lb) manual, 1,385kg (3,054lb) automatic
Max power	150bhp @ 5,900rpm
Max torque	140lb ft (190Nm) @ 3,500rpm
Top speed	130mph (209km/h) manual, 128mph (206km/h) automatic
0–62mph	8.9sec manual, 9.9sec automatic

★ Some early cars fitted four-speed automatic gearbox

The Smallest Six

By taking the 2-litre engine from the 520, the Z3 development team was able to offer potential customers the choice of a six-cylinder model at a much lower price than had previously been available. The new (at least to the Z3 Series) powerplant displaced 1,991cc, with short-stroke bore and stroke dimensions of 80 × 66mm respectively. Maximum power was 150bhp, with torque figures of 140lb ft (190Nm) at 3,500rpm; maximum speed was a claimed 130mph (209km/h). The 0–62mph (0–100km/h) acceleration figure of 8.9sec was dented when the cost-option automatic gearbox was specified, losing a full 1sec: 9.9sec.

The new double VANOS engine of the revised 2.8 six. Although power output at 193bhp remained unchanged, maximum torque was produced at 3,500rpm, instead of 3,950rpm on the outgoing model!

Speedster humps fitted to a 2000 Z3 2.8. This car is also fitted with 17in, cross-spoke, split-rim alloy wheels.

As regards performance, the 2.0 six didn't appear to offer much of an advantage over the new 1,895cc, '1.8', four-cylinder model. The entry-level six also cost exactly £3,000 more, at £22,995. However, beside the prestige of six cylinders, buyers got alloy wheels (16in, five-star spoke type, with 225/50 ZR16 tyres), front fog lights, M Sport steering wheel, and twin exhaust tail-pipes.

Fuel consumption, compared to the four-cylinder model, dropped by some 6mpg.

The revised Z3s can be identified instantly by the new-type light assembly shown here.

Side view of the revised Z3 Series showing the new rear section of the fluted wings.

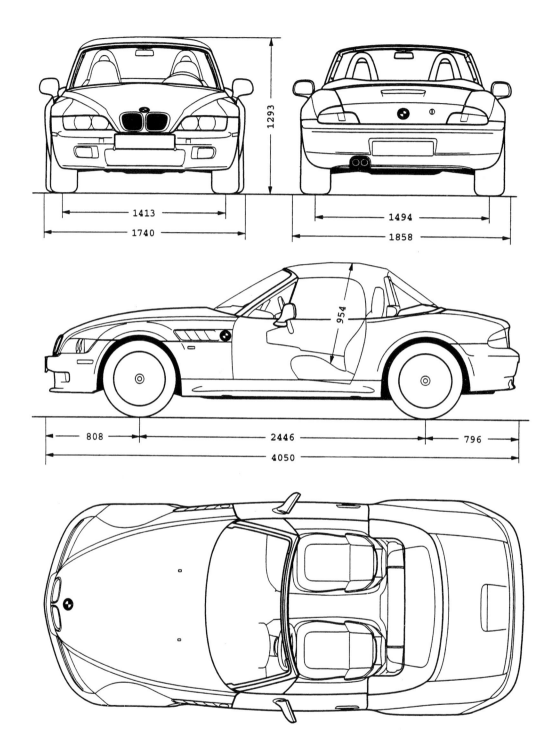

Dimension drawings showing the 2000 model revisions (the M Series cars remained unchanged). The measurements given are in millimetres.

The changes were to the styling, engines and interior; the chassis, however, was not touched, so the Z3 remained more a cruiser than a sports car.

The Uprated 2.8

The performance of the 2.8 model was further improved thanks to double instead of single VANOS variable valve timing. Although outright power, at 193bhp, was the same as the

Rear view of a 2000 model Z3 2.8. The new styling is evident in this view. On the 2.8 there were chrome exhaust trims (black on 2.0 model). This car has the optional speedster humps.

outgoing model, maximum torque was produced lower down the range at 3,500rpm (instead of 3,950rpm). Compared to the 2.0 six, the revised 2.8 featured:

- Alloy wheels with eight-star spokes;
- Chrome-plated exhaust tail-pipes;
- Electrically powered roof;
- Height-adjustable passenger seat;
- Limited slip differential;
- On-board computer;
- Leather upholstery;
- Rear roll-over bars.

The boot-lid release now had this extension, making opening an easier task than on earlier cars (it had formally been an optional extra).

The UK price had been increased from £28,145 to £28,350.

Exterior Styling Changes
Besides the undoubted improvements to the car's technical and equipment specifications, the Z3 updated models also featured revised styling. The bodywork at the rear of all the cars outlined above (but not the M Series) had been given a wider, more purposeful appearance. New rear wings were wider and more curved than previously, giving a more balanced effect between the nose and tail.

The interior benefited from additional chrome, revised seats, new-style steering wheel and revised centre console switches.

A post-2000 Z3 with optional hard top. Manufactured in aluminium, it is easily fitted and comes complete with a heated rear glass window (plastic on the soft roof). The hard top is available in the full range of Z3 colours, and cost around £2,000 in the UK (2003 prices).

The rear tail-lights had been changed to the classic L-shape found on many of BMW's other models. At the front, chrome rings emphasized the dual headlights. There were four new paint colours to choose from:

- Sienna Red;
- Topaz Blue;
- Impala Brown;
- Steel Grey.

Interior Styling Changes

On the inside, the revised Z3 featured a new instrument layout, a colour-coded centre console, and a choice of no fewer than six new interior trims.

A round clock with a chrome ring, to match the heater controls, now sat in the centre of the console. There were also new switches, shared with the M Roadster, whilst the controls for the electric hood (where fitted) were now positioned between the seats, to leave the dashboard less cluttered.

ABOVE AND BELOW: The Z3 Series has proved one of BMW's best sellers as regards cost and extra goodies, many owners wishing to make their car as unique as possible. The range of equipment is truly vast, from body kits to hi-fi systems, chrome accessories to heated seats.

Included in the options list are chrome door handles.

Heated seats (switches bottom right and bottom left).

More costly options include the hard top...

...and speedster humps.

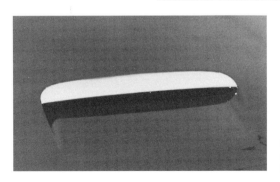

Post-2000 model year cars – eight-valve 1,895cc '1.8', 2.0, 2.2, 2.8 (double VANOS) and 3.0 – can be fitted with chrome trim for the third brake light.

The new colours/interior trim/upholstery options meant up to twenty combinations, there being four materials: flat-weave cloth, Z-Tex imitation leather, Oregon leather and Classic leather. Both Classic and Oregon leather could be extended to include the door trims, dashboard and centre console. In each case the centre console panel was colour-coded to match the interior. Matt chrome and maple wood were also available as options.

Technically Speaking

From a purely technical viewpoint it is important to point out that the revised models did not change significantly from the models they replaced in areas such as chassis, body rigidity, steering or braking. However, it is worth noting

For the 2001 model year (from mid-2000) the 2.0 was replaced by the 2.2. This had 20bhp more, and the engine size was increased from 1,991cc to 2,171cc. Torque was increased from 140lb ft (190Nm) to 152lb ft (210Nm).

that the 2.0 six shared the ventilated front discs previously used on the 2.8 models of the original series.

<table>
<tr><td colspan="2" align="center">**The Z3 2.2 Roadster (2001)**</td></tr>
<tr><td>Engine</td><td>Liquid-cooled, twenty-four-valve, dohc, inline, six-cylinder with single VANOS</td></tr>
<tr><td>Displacement</td><td>2,171cc</td></tr>
<tr><td>Bore</td><td>80mm</td></tr>
<tr><td>Stroke</td><td>72mm</td></tr>
<tr><td>Compression ratio</td><td>10.8:1</td></tr>
<tr><td>Transmission</td><td>Five-speed, manual; five-speed, Steptronic automatic</td></tr>
<tr><td>Doors</td><td>Two</td></tr>
<tr><td>Seats</td><td>Two</td></tr>
<tr><td>Chassis</td><td>Unitary construction</td></tr>
<tr><td>Bodywork</td><td>Steel, galvanized, with bolt-on panels</td></tr>
<tr><td>Suspension</td><td>Front: spring-strut front axle with anti-dive and anti-roll bar
Rear: semi-trailing arm rear axle, anti-squat and anti-dive; anti-roll bar.</td></tr>
<tr><td>Drive</td><td>Rear wheel</td></tr>
<tr><td>Wheels</td><td>Cast alloy 7J × 16 front and rear</td></tr>
<tr><td>Tyres</td><td>225/50 R-16 front and rear</td></tr>
<tr><td>*Dimensions*</td><td></td></tr>
<tr><td>Overall length</td><td>4,050mm (159in)</td></tr>
<tr><td>Overall width</td><td>1,740mm (68.5in)</td></tr>
<tr><td>Overall height</td><td>1,293mm (51in)</td></tr>
<tr><td>Wheelbase</td><td>2,446mm (96.3in)</td></tr>
<tr><td>Dry weight</td><td>1,345kg (2,966lb) manual, 1,385kg (3,054lb) automatic</td></tr>
<tr><td>Max power</td><td>170bhp @ 6,250rpm</td></tr>
<tr><td>Max torque</td><td>152lb ft (210Nm) @ 3,550rpm</td></tr>
<tr><td>Top speed</td><td>139mph (224km/h) manual, 137mph (221km/h) automatic</td></tr>
<tr><td>0–62mph</td><td>7.9sec manual, 8.9sec automatic</td></tr>
</table>

The Z3 3.0 Roadster (2001)

Engine	Liquid-cooled, twenty-four-valve, dohc, inline, six-cylinder with single VANOS
Displacement	2,797cc
Bore	84mm
Stroke	89.6mm
Compression ratio	10.2:1
Transmission	Five-speed, manual/five-speed, Steptronic automatic
Doors	Two
Seats	Two
Chassis	Unitary construction
Bodywork	Steel, galvanized, with bolt-on panels
Suspension	Front: spring-strut front axle with anti-dive and anti-roll bar
	Rear: semi-trailing arm rear axle, anti-squat and anti-dive; anti-roll bar
Drive	Rear wheel
Wheels	Cast alloy 7J × 16 front and rear
Tyres	225/50 R-16 front and rear

Dimensions

Overall length	4,050mm (159in)
Overall width	1,740mm (68.5in)
Overall height	1,293mm (51in)
Wheelbase	2,446mm (96.3in)
Dry weight	1,360kg (2,999lb) manual, 1,400kg (3,087lb) automatic
Max power	231bhp @ 5,900rpm
Max torque	224lb ft (300Nm) @ 3,500rpm
Top speed	150mph (241km/h) manual, 147mph (237km/h) automatic
0–62mph	6sec manual, 6.3sec automatic

Interior from the 2001 Z3 2.2 model.

Also new for the 2001 model year was the 3.0 model, with the 2,979cc M54 engine putting out 231bhp.

The 3.0 badge proclaimed that from a power point of view, this is the nearest to the M Series engine yet, with 231bhp on top.

The Z3 Sport Models

For the 2001 model year (autumn 2000 onwards), BMW launched sport versions of its 2.2 and 3.0 Z3 models. Unfortunately these were not true sports versions, more a cosmetic marketing exercise.

BMW's brochure stated 'The Z3 Sport Roadster. Available with 2.2-litre or 3.0-litre powerplants, the models combine enhanced exterior styling with a more sport-orientated interior. Distinctive alloy wheels and aggressive front air-intake with mesh grille are married to lowered sports suspension, giving a more dynamic presence on the road. In the cabin, the driver will find increased lateral support from the sculptured sports seats, and increased tactility from the M leather steering wheel and gear knob. The following are Z3 sport model features:

- Front air dam;
- Sports suspension, with uprated spring and damper setting. Limited slip differential on both 2.2 and 3.0 models;
- Cross-spoke style 78 alloy wheel, size 7.5J × 17 front and 8.5J × 17 rear. Tyre size of 225/45 front and 245/40 rear;
- Brushed aluminium centre console;
- Sports seats with chameleon leather upholstery; heated seats;
- M leather steering wheel;
- White lens for third brake light.'

Maybe BMW should have labelled these versions 'de luxe' rather than 'sport', the latter tending to give a rather misleading impression of a higher performance than the standard version.

The UK prices of the sport models (spring 2001) were: Z3 2.2i Sports Roadster, £23,230 (Std model £21,840); Z3 3.3i Sports Roadster, £27,730 (Std model £26,930).

ABOVE RIGHT: *The 2001 model year saw the introduction of the 2.2- and 3.0-litre Sport models. These came with sports suspension, 17in cross-spoke alloy wheels, a new front air dam with wire mesh, revised interior, and a white lens for third brake light.*

RIGHT: *Interior of the 2001 Z3 Sport model, with aluminium-effect central console, leather M steering wheel, and leather sports seating.*

Developing the M54 3.0-Litre Engine

BMW engineers took a mere twenty-four months to develop their 2,979cc 3-litre dohc straight-six power unit. Utilizing the aluminium crankcase and cast liners from the outgoing 2.8, the new 3-litre benefited from an increase in stroke – up from 84 to 89.6mm – and a newly designed crankshaft. The opening period of the inlet valves was also extended, whilst valve lift was increased.

The BMW engineering team had also carried out detailed modifications to the company's double VANOS variable camshaft timing. And to improve both throttle response and smoothness, the electro-mechanical throttle was replaced by a fully electronic version carried over from BMW's own V12 powerplant.

Engineers had also spent development time improving gas flow rates for both the inlet and exhaust ports. And thanks to a reduction in piston friction, a lower engine idle speed and

Introduced in mid-2000, the new M54 dohc, in-line, six-cylinder engine that powers the Z3 3.0, displaces 2,979cc and produces 231bhp.

optimization of the valve timing, the increase in engine size and power output had been achieved without affecting fuel consumption as compared with the outgoing 2.8 engine.

Maintenance costs, as on most modern BMW production engines, had also been a priority, so items such as air filters and spark plugs are designed to last 62,000 miles (100,000km). As on the 2.8, the 3.0 also benefits from a service indicator that calculates the distance remaining before an oil service is due.

Finally, the M54 3.0 engine automatically adjusts to run on fuel octane ratings between 87 and 98 octane, although BMW sources say that it will only produce all its 231bhp when given 98 octane Super Plus unleaded.

The awesome M54 2,979cc (84 × 89.6mm), dohc, fuel-injected straight-six engine. It generates an impressive 231bhp, with the maximum torque of 219lb ft (300Nm) at 3,500rpm.

The 3.0-litre Z3 can accelerate from 0–62mph (100km/h) in a mere 6sec. But the chassis struggles with all that power far more than the outgoing 2.8 version.

The Grip Factor

The Z3 Series has often been accused of having too much grip for its own good. The general feeling amongst the motoring press is that in a racing car, acres of grip is essential; on road cars, however, it is not always the most important indicator of a fun drive.

In their 1 August 2001 issue, *Autocar* staged what they called the 'Grip Challenge'. This produced some very interesting results, and although pitted against the Lotus Elise, which came fourth overall in the twenty-four-car test, the Z3 (a 3.0 model) came out an excellent ninth. *Autocar* also found the Z3 'wonderfully stable', and although beaten by the Elise, *Autocar* called the Z3 performance 'a solid result'.

Autocar's Grip Challenge results

1st	Formula Palmer (race car)	13th	Mini Cooper (2001 model)
2nd	Noble M12	14th	Nissan Almera Tino
3rd	Porsche 911 (cup tyres)	15th	Audi A4 quattro
4th	Lotus Elise	16th	Seat Ibiza Cupra R
5th	Mitsubishi Evo VII	17th	Nissan Almera Saloon
6th	Lotus 340R	18th	Land Rover Discovery
7th	BMW 330	19th	Nissan Almera Hatch
8th	Suburu Impreza UK300	20th	Land Rover Discovery ACE
9th	BMW Z3 3.0	21st	Volvo S60
10th	Porsche 911 (road tyres)	22nd	Honda Insight
11th	Renault Clio 172	23rd	MCC Smart
12th	Fiat Seicento Sporting	24th	Citroën 2CV

Considering the opposition, both the Z3 3.0 and the 330 saloon put in a good performance for BMW. You would probably have to be driving at 10/10ths to unstick either, unless the car was suffering from faulty tyres or suspension. *Autocar* obviously considered the test of considerable importance saying:

> For the first time in this magazine's 106-year history, we've managed to generate meaningful data about cornering, which means from this point on it won't just be our backsides telling us what's what when it comes to handling assessment. We'll also use our new g-meter in major road tests.

One of the 3.0 Z3 models, with AC Schnitzer front spoiler, Type III alloy wheels, M3-type mirrors and chrome roll-over bars.

A 2002 model year Z3 3.0, equipped with BMW accessories including full body kit, chrome line exterior, 17in radial spoke composite 86 wheels, Speedster humps and M-mirrors.

Steptronic Auto Transmission

From the year 2000, the six-cylinder models (excluding the M variants) had the option of the excellent Steptronic gearbox, in place of the standard five-speed manual. When required, it converts the BMW five-speed EH automatic transmission into a clutchless manual set-up. To operate Steptronic, you simply move the selector lever from position D (automatic model) into sports programme 'S'.

For individual gear selection in position 'S' you push – in fact best described as a nudge – the selector lever forwards to upshift, and backwards to downshift. The selected gear is then displayed in the instrument panel. Steptronic even allows the driver to drop down a gear or two before overtaking, or to flick to a lower gear for engine breaking prior to entering a corner.

The new Steptronic auto gearbox also benefited from AGS (adaptive transmission control) and shiftlock. AGS is a programme that constantly adapts the character of the car to the road conditions and the way in which it is being driven. It measures whether the car is going up- or downhill; how hard the car is being cornered; how slippery the road surface is; it knows if the sports 'S' programme has been selected; it even knows if the car is stuck in heavy traffic. Then it works out which of the programmes is the most appropriate, and selects the gear that provides the kind of performance you want. In addition, AGS is programmed to adapt the gearchange pattern for mountains, starting off, severe bends, stop/go traffic and winter driving. If the accelerator pedal is depressed gently, AGS will choose extra economy. More determined pressure or quick release will select extra sport instantly. Unless 'S' sport mode is selected, AGS will always choose the most economical programme for the conditions.

It has no memory – instead it reacts constantly to whoever is driving the car and to changes in the driving conditions. AGS means a Z3 with this system can be a relaxed cruiser or a sports car or anything in between.

For safety reasons, the shiftlock on BMW automatic transmissions ensures that from selector lever positions 'N' or 'P' a drive position can only be selected when the brake pedal is depressed. Interlock is a safety feature of BMW auto transmissions that prevents the ignition key from being removed from the ignition unless you have moved the selector lever into position 'P'.

The new five-speed Steptronic gearbox with AGS (Adaptive Gearbox System). This could be specified as an option in place of the manual five-speed box on the 2.2 and 3.0 Z3 models. It was introduced for the Z3s from autumn 2000.

Top Seller

The 2.0 model was the best seller of the new series in Britain during 1990, accounting for around 40 per cent of sales. The balance was shared by the 2.8 and 1.8 at between 25–30 per cent each, whereas the unchanged M roadster accounted for a much smaller 3 per cent of the market.

The 2.2 and 3.0 Models Join the Range

For the 2001 model year (beginning in late summer 2000) BMW replaced the 2.0 and 2.8 models with the new 2.2 and 3.0 versions. The 2.2 displaced 2,171cc (80 × 72mm) and produced 170bhp, whereas the 3.0 figures were 2,979cc (84 × 89.6mm) and 231bhp. Both these had significantly more outright power, but again the chassis design was not altered to any degree to offset the extra power. This meant that in the 3.0 model at least, the engine's performance was in excess of the chassis' ability to handle it – if using full performance.

Testing the Newcomers

Out on the road, the new 3 litre with 150mph (240km/h) and 0–62mph (0–100km/h) of 6.0sec almost matched that of the M version. However, it was the new 2.2-litre car that really impressed, its 170bhp (as opposed to the large-

Interior of the 2002 model 3.0.

Z3 Showroom Winner

By the time the Z3's replacement was publicly announced in July 2002, a total of almost 300,000 Z3 Series cars had been sold. So whatever else the motoring press could throw at the model, showroom success was not one of them, with the Z3 being by far and away the most popular BMW roadster of all time. As this book reveals, it is essentially a useable, comfortable, everyday cruiser that can double up as a sports car. What it most certainly is not, is a raw-boned sports car of the old school, with little or no comfort, and performance and handling as its sole priority. The Z3 is a much broader-based vehicle, which together with its build quality, BMW badge, retro looks and range of models – and price structure – meant that it became a massive sales success. Quite simply, whatever the press may have thought, the Z3 has had the buyer's vote with their own money – what better recommendation can you have? And to be absolutely honest, this is in stark contrast to road-test favourites such as the 507 and Z1, which both proved poor sellers.

The Z3 has also proved that BMW can still build quality cars, even if they are produced in a newly constructed factory, many thousands of miles from the company's Munich headquarters and on another continent.

engined car's 231bhp) being far happier in the Z3's chassis. In fact, together with the now-axed 2.8, the 2.2 is, in the author's opinion, the best of the Z3 Series. In performance terms it can reach 139mph (224km/h), and it can accelerate from 0–62mph in 7.9sec (8.9sec in automatic).

Both the 2.2 and the 3.0 came with double VANOS variable valve timing. In addition, a Steptronic five-speed automatic was a cost option for both cars. This was a massive improvement over the old four-speed automatic gearbox of the previous Z3 generation, allowing the driver to use not only the auto mode, but also the manual: by flicking the 'box' into manual form, upward and downward changes can be effected by simply touching the gearstick (these changes of course being clutchless). The BMW Steptronic really is a brilliant system, and both the 2.2 and 3.0 engines proved equally suitable.

The extra 180cc from the old 2.0 litre may not seem very much but the combination of 20bhp more, and improved torque through the use of double VANOS transformed the smaller sixes' performance. And combined with the Steptronic gearbox, it is delightful. In addition, when using the Steptronic unit with the 3.0-litre engine, a mere 0.3sec is traded off, as compared to the manual 'box' in the 0–62mph figures…very impressive indeed. I, for one, wouldn't consider a manual box on the 3.0. Get yourself a 3-litre Z3 auto, and it fully lives up to its 'ultimate cruiser' tag. If you go for the manual 'box', you would be better off with a softer 2.8 model.

Summary

A total of 297,087 Z3s of all models had been built by the time production ceased in spring 2002. And there had been no significant changes after the end of 2000, for the 2001 model year production. This meant that the four-cylinder models did not benefit from the introduction of the new British-made (Hams Hall, Birmingham factory), sixteen-valve, Valvetronic power units that were first put into the new E46 316/318Ti Compact models that appeared in mid-2001; these power units were also incorporated into the 2002 3 Series saloon range a few months later. Moreover, at the time of writing it is not clear if the Z3's replacement, the Z4, will feature four-cylinder engines in its line-up: in late 2002 at the Z4's official launch, only 2.5- and 3.0-litre, six-cylinder models were mentioned.

During its seven-year production life the Z3 was shown to be an excellent all-rounder, capable of a wide range of roles. What it most certainly was not was a narrow-focused sports car. Those who purchased their Z3 new, as well as those who bought theirs in the used car market, will have found that, in common with other BMWs, their cars have a superb reliability record.

My own personal favourites in the Z3 range were the M Coupé, the original 2.8 six-cylinder, the 2001 2.2, and of the four-cylinder models the 8-valve 1.9 litre '1.8'. Of course this is only *my* choice, though it is based on having driven every model in the range. Again on a personal note, I found the M Roadster not in the same handling league as the M Coupé; the 3.0 six stretching the chassis more than the 2.8; whilst the sixteen-valve 1.9 was a bit too rev-happy for my liking.

Owning a Z3 is very much a case of appreciating its virtues, whilst accepting its weaknesses – so with the right model, it is still an excellent car that can perform a wide range of tasks with considerable ability. And with the number of cars and its good reliability record, the Z3 seems set to be a familiar sight for many years to come.

11   Prototypes

Running alongside the various production Z Series cars have been numerous prototypes. Quite often these have remained for company use only, not being displayed in public, and in many cases have not been particularly sporting or even attractive, but mainly serving as a mobile testbed for new ideas or technology.

The Z1

The first of the Zs was the Z1 (*see* Chapter 3), and it was the very first project for the newly formed BMW-Technik organization. In retrospect it was the Z1 that was the trendsetter for the modern roadster revival, not the generally acknowledged Japanese Mazda MX5.

The Z1 project was largely the responsibility of chief engineer Dipl. Ing. Ulrich Bez and former Ford Europe man, Harm Laggay. Dr Bez was also responsible for a Z3-like roadster (on paper only) that was intended as a combined BMW–Porsche venture, using different body shapes on a shared floor plan. This latter project was never given a code number. Although the press got to see the Z1 'prototype' in August 1986, there were by then two vehicles: one a working prototype, the other a styling mock-up.

As the Z1 story in Chapter 3 reveals, the car featured several innovations, at least for BMW, such as an all-plastic body, vertically sliding doors, monocoque chassis, an all-new rear suspension system, plus an undershield system that provided ground-effect, with negative lift front and rear. A little known fact is that four-wheel drive was also considered, but was ultimately ditched for a number of reasons – notably the fact that BMW considered it 'futuristic' and outside company mainstream policy!

By 1986 the Z1 wheelbase had been increased by 52mm (2in) for what was to become the production version. But both prototype and production cars featured lightweight integrated plastic bumpers, crash-proof up to a speed of 5mph.

At the time, BMW sources described the Z1 as a 'fun car – a contrast to the carefully developed, mass-produced family saloon'. But there is little doubt that the Z1 (like the later Z8) also served an important role in developing BMW technology. For example, the Z1's multi-link rear suspension was subsequently used in mainstream models, including the new E36 3 Series from 1990.

The A.R. Penck Z1

One Z1 came finished in a very non-standard paint job: it was actually used as a 'canvas' by the well-known artist A.R. Penck. Something of a BMW tradition, this use of the car as a mobile art form was begun back in 1975 with Hervé Poulain racing a 3-litre CSL Coupé, painted by Alexander Calder.

Subsequently, many famous artists, including Fuchs, Lichtenstein and Warhol, have all practised their art on BMWs. The Penck Z1 was decorated in a mass of black abstract symbols and was created in 1991; it was the eleventh BMW 'art car', and the first to be painted by a German artist.

The X Coupé

Although the X Coupé concept car of 2001 was never officially given a Z code number, it nonetheless is a prototype that plays a supporting role in this book's story – and which points the way forward for BMW. Why? Well, styling boss Chris Bangle has 'spent the last few years upsetting the artfully constructed BMW design applecart', as the August 2002 edition of *Car* so correctly puts it. *Car* again:

> Everyone was happy with the current 3 Series, but he [Bangle] and his team then upended the consensus with the Z9 concept in both Coupé and roadster forms. The X Coupé (which had very strong Fiat Coupé overtones – a previous Bangle concoction) had the press demanding his head on a stake.

ABOVE: *The X Coupé concept car of 2001 was the first to use Chris Bangle's controversial convex and concave styling, with its mixture of rounded and sharp lines, together with the squared-off wheel arches, which were to be such a feature of the Z4 when it was launched a few months later in mid-2002.*

LEFT: *The interior of the X Coupé was minimalistic, with the driver having, in effect, his (or her) own compartment. Again, as on the Z18, the dials were of the retro-styled circular pattern. The rim of the steering wheel was of the chamois-leather variety.*

continued overleaf

The X Coupé *continued*

Finally, the man from *Car* points out that Chris Bangle is 'an ultra-confident American who comes across as the most popular lecturer on the campus – and he was unmoved.'

So, is Bangle right to be so confident in his abilities? Only time will tell if, ultimately, he is branded a hero or a villain. And of course it will not be the press who will be the ultimate judge of this, but the buying customer. In other words, Bangle could be hailed in the same terms as Sir Alex Ferguson, or soon become the next Premier League sacking.

Bangle's 'flame-surfacing' styling did not get off to the best of starts with its debut in the X Coupé. However, whatever one may think, it is a significant step in the evolution of the BMW's styling – providing, of course, it sets a successful trend.

Already the Z4 has been launched (*see* Chapter 14) and we are promised the 1 Series range, plus another Bangle styling job, the next generation 5 Series. All these take inspiration from the 2000 X Coupé concept, and their success or otherwise will not only have an effect on Chris Bangle's own reign at BMW, but the German company's continued financial health in future years. But I seem to remember the Fiat Coupé did not do much to restore Fiat's fortunes...

It is debatable if the rearward-opening section of the X Coupé shown here would have been practical in use. Also the styling of the car was not very popular, even though some features are likely to be seen in future BMW design trends, notably the forthcoming 1 Series.

The Z2 Project

Actually coming after the Z3, the Z2 project (which may still see the light of day) was first revealed towards the end of the 1990s. It was considerably smaller than its older brother, and could have been ready for launch in the autumn of 2002. To reduce costs, it employed the platform and engines from the outgoing Compact model. This fixed the wheelbase, engine mounting points and windscreen position. Even so, a design team led by the Z9's concept creator,

Chris Bangle, had, BMW sources revealed, managed to make the Z2 look stunning. There were two bodies: the 2 + 2 Coupé or two-seater roadster.

The original Z2 (codenamed E46/5-S) aimed to attract a younger clientele, something BMW saw as important to its future growth. And, as outlined in Chapter 14, the Z2 project has been updated and given a new codename: E82/2. The 'new' Z2 will share the rear-wheel-drive platform of the forthcoming 1 Series, and should go on sale in late 2006.

The latest incarnation of the Z2 is meant to complement the newly introduced Z4, and will sport Chris Bangle's controversial 'flame-surfacing' design, with intersecting convex and concave surfaces and dramatically different lines. Buyers can count on the classic roadster proportions of a long bonnet and snub rear, with a manual cloth hood. Power will come from BMW's four-cylinder Valvetronic petrol engine, and to keep the price down there are no six-cylinder engines planned. Even the flagship M version will feature a 2.2 tuned four, with a magnesium cylinder block. The latest Z2 project is expected to compete head-on with the upcoming Mercedes.

Z3 Prototypes

There were several Z3 prototypes, but BMW has steadfastly refused to allow details or pictures. In fact the Z3 project was one of the most closely guarded in the German company's long history. Some of this centred around the controversial location where production was subsequently to take place, North America. What is definite is that BMW prepared two running prototypes to act in a supporting role for 007 James Bond in the blockbuster film, *Goldeneye* (1995). In fact BMW had signed a contract to provide vehicles for three Bond movies, and the subsequent films, *Tomorrow Never Dies* (1997) and *The World is Not Enough* (1998), starred a 750i saloon and an R1200C motorcycle, and a Z8 respectively.

The Z07 project

In the autumn of 1997, the world had its first view of BMW's Z07 concept car when the wraps were taken off at the Tokyo Motor Show. At the time the car was hailed as the prototype successor to the legendary Albrecht Goertz-designed 507 Roadster of the late 1950s.

As for the Z07's production version, the Z8, which followed in 2000, the designer was a young Dane, Henrik Fisker.

The Z07 prototype made its bow at the Tokyo Motor Show in autumn 1997. It was designed by the young Dane, Henrik Fisker, who used the BMW 507 as inspiration.

The interior of the Z07 concept car was very similar to the one used by BMW when building its new Z8 model.

The Z07 looked right from any angle. In this three-quarters rear view it is possible to see more Z8 styling cues, such as the rear lights and twin exhausts.

The Z07 Coupé was almost Aston Martin in the treatment of the roofline. Unfortunately, with BMW's ditching of the retro look, a similar production car seems an impossible dream.

The links with the past and the Z07 were very clear, with key elements including the trademark grille, along with the classically styled chromed side air ducts.

The Z07 was displayed in both roadster and Coupé forms. As yet, BMW has not offered a Z8 Coupé, only the roadster.

When the Z8 entered production, much of the running gear was sourced from the M5 spare parts bin, but the same could not be said of the interior. This was, in the main, truly bespoke, and it became instantly apparent that BMW had taken the bold (and unusual) step of retaining many of the original features of the Z07 show vehicle. This included the beautifully retro-styled, spoked steering wheel, and the instrument console that sat in the middle of the dashboard, angled towards the driver; giving the cabin a particularly classy look.

The Z11

The Z11, more commonly known as the E1 (the 'E' standing for 'Electric'), was first announced in 1991. BMW Technik had built the car in response to the parent company's long-standing desire to develop an electric vehicle. Technik's engineers were quick to realize that, due to battery weight and range, the only viable role for an electric car was to produce a small, purpose-built city vehicle. Until then, BMW had attempted to convert existing products, notably 3 Series saloons, to electric propulsion – without, it must be said, much success. These attempts had been made over almost two decades, from the first attempt in 1972, until the end of the 1980s.

The Z11 (E1) was only ever intended as a prototype. It is maybe worth mentioning that besides using simply batteries, another version was envisaged using hybrid power sources (similar to the Honda Insight and Toyota Pirus): this would have used a motorcycle engine in addition to batteries.

The Z13

Coded Z13, the second-generation electric city car would probably have entered production, had it not been for BMW's purchase of the British Rover Group in January 1994.

The Z13 had been publicly announced ten months earlier at the Geneva Motor Show in March 1993, and it was subsequently displayed on the company's stand at eleven more exhibitions, including making its debut at the Frankfurt Motor Show in September 1993 (two years after the Z11, the original BMW

electric car, had been rolled out at Frankfurt in September 1991).

Besides the Z11 hybrid version described earlier, there were two prototypes of the Z13: one had only battery power but, with a power output of 10kwh, it could reach 78mph (125km/h) and had a maximum range of 165 miles (265km); the other was petrol only, and was powered by a BMW K1100 motorcycle-derived unit – the liquid-cooled, dohc, sixteen-valve, in-line four produced 81bhp and offered a maximum speed of 112mph (180km/h), 0–62mph (100km/h) in 11.5sec, and 40–50mpg (7–5.7ltr/100km) fuel economy.

The Z13 was the work of BMW Technik's English designer Robert Powell (who had

Just two prototypes of the Z13 were built. The car shown here is the first prototype and was originally intended to have automatic transmission, but ended up with a five-speed manual gearbox. It made its public debut at the Frankfurt Motor Show in September 1993. And although it was shown at a further eleven shows and created a good deal of positive publicity, the purchase of the Rover Group in early 1994, and the subsequent development of the new Mini, effectively sealed the Z13's fate.

begun his career at the old Austin-Rover company during the early 1980s) and incorporated some radical thinking. Its power unit (in the definitive motorcycle-only engined version) was mounted centrally in the car and drove the rear wheels, this set-up providing a nearly ideal front-to-rear weight distribution. The Z13 featured three, rather than four, seats, the driver sitting in the middle of the car, ahead of two passengers who, in this way, enjoyed much improved legroom than would otherwise have been possible. The down side to this layout was a lack of luggage space, but this was considered not to be a major issue in a car intended mainly for short-haul city work.

A comprehensive road-test programme was carried out, which revealed excellent on-road dynamics: *BMW Car* in their February 1995 issue reported 'The car feels much more like a sports machine than a hot hatchback' – but the Z13 was ultimately ditched in favour of the new Mini. And with the success of the latter car, it has to be said that BMW probably made the right decision from both a commercial and vehicle viewpoint.

The Z14

The Z14 was not a car at all, but entered production in 2000 as the CI scooter! But to many two-wheel enthusiasts the CI was in reality a two-wheel car. If all this is confusing, let me explain. BMW Technik showed their usual flair for innovation, but in the CI's case, it was not for performance, handling or even good looks: instead it attempted to address a safety issue. This was by way of providing an aluminium frame that formed an all-round safety cell and at the same time doubled as a roll-over bar. In addition, a roof and windscreen were provided. All these features are probably good, sensible ideas for either a scooter or even a motorcycle. However – and here comes the crunch – scooterists and

motorcyclists are extremely conservative, with the result that the CI (Z14) has proved a poor seller. Also, at a retail price of around £4,500 in the UK, rival 125cc (the CI's engine size) machines are much cheaper. But those who have purchased a CI have taken delivery of a machine featuring a four-stroke, single-cylinder engine producing 15bhp, a digital engine management system, an infinitely viable automatic belt-drive transmission, a catalytic converter, anti-dive front suspension, monoshock rear suspension, together with ABS and dual windscreen wipers as standard equipment. But it has to be said that BMW Technik failed to study other advanced vehicles that have proved showroom flops, including the Bimota Tesi, Yamaha 1000 GTS and the Ariel 3 trike, not to mention the infamous Sinclair C5.

The Z18

The Z18 was inspired by one of BMW's most successful motorcycles of recent years, the R1100 G/S (a cross between a touring bike and an off-road racer); it was designed by BMW Technik to 'combine the driving appeal of a roadster with the strength and high seating position of an off-road vehicle'.

Destined to remain a prototype only, the Z18 was first constructed back in 1995, but it was not until five years later, in 2000, that its existence was made known. One journalist described it as having 'a boat-like body', but it was actually designed this way to allow variable configurations: thus the Z18 could have been a two-seater off-beat roadster, a two-seat pick-up, or a 2-plus-2 with the convenience of a boot.

The Z18 made use of the 4.4-litre V8 powerplant found in some versions of the X5. But as the Z18 weighed in at some two-thirds the weight of an X5, performance was brisk, to say the least.

The instruments of the Z18 were positioned centrally, and clearly followed classic motorcycle and car design. The interior was similar to other recent Z prototypes, and was reasonably conventional, retro even.

BELOW: The Z18 used a four-wheel-drive system similar to that of the X5 all-terrain vehicle introduced in 1998. Like some versions of the X5, the Z18 was powered by a 4.4-litre V8 engine.

Like the Z22 saloon, the Z18 all-terrain Roadster project was not revealed until 2000, even though it had existed since 1995. The Z18 was designed to combine the driving enjoyment of the Roadster, but with the strength and high seating position of an off-road vehicle. Its inspiration had in fact come from BMW's successful R1100 G/S enduro motorcycle – the latter being a cross between a touring bike and a motocross machine.

It sported a quartet of small, close-fitting mudguards that were completely divorced from the main body shell. There were also four individual circular headlamps. Even so, the Z18 managed to retain the corporate BMW style, whilst the interior was notable for a trio of white-faced, centrally positioned instruments that would not have been out of place on a classic car or motorcycle. The balance of the interior, when compared to other recent Z Series prototypes, was fairly conventional, even retro.

But ultimately, even for BMW, the all-terrain roadster was simply a step too far.

Maybe it is a concept that will be followed through to production by another manufacturer some time in the future.

The Z21

The Z21 label was applied to a strange mixture of car and motorcycle technologies; it made its debut at the 1995 Tokyo Show as the Just 4/2. Essentially the Z21 was BMW Technik's view of what a motorcycle on four wheels should look like.

The Z21 (more commonly known as the Just 4/2) was announced at the 1995 Tokyo Motor Show. The '4/2' tag was intended to convey BMW Technik's intention of effectively producing a motorcycle on four wheels. Weighing in at 550kg (1,212lb), power came from the 100bhp, BMW, K1100, four-cylinder motorcycle engine mounted in the rear.

Powered by a rear-mounted BMW 1,100cc, liquid-cooled, sixteen-valve, dohc, in-line, four-cylinder, fuel-injected engine, the Z21 weighed in at a meagre 550kg (1,213lb). With 100bhp on tap, this meant that the engine could reach 0–62mph (100km/h) in 6sec, making it a particularly rapid device.

Even though no roof or windscreen were provided, there was a high level of safety equipment, including driver and passenger airbags, a roll-over bar, side-impact protection and, as cost options, weatherproof clothing and helmets. Innovations included a boot compartment that could be detached and used as a suitcase.

In many ways the Z21 (Just 4/2) was BMW's answer to the likes of the Caterham or Westfield; but unlike its British rivals, the BMW did not get offered to the buying public, even though it was a much more modern design.

The Z21 (Just 4/2) was a strange mixture of the spartan (no roof or windscreen) and the sophisticated (a high level of safety equipment, which included airbags for both driver and passenger, as well as side-impact bars).

The Z22 saloon was revealed in 2000, to celebrate the fifteenth anniversary of BMW Technik GmbH; the project had begun back in 1995. The aim was to produce a car that had the comfort of a 5 Series, the carrying capacity of the 5 Series Tourer, whilst employing automatic transmission and the ability to average 6ltr of fuel per 100km (39mpg). It also had to achieve stringent safety, environmental and re-cycling standards. The Z22 made use of CFK (carbon-fibre reinforced plastic) in its structure.

The Z22

Announced in 2000, the Z22 was, BMW said, 'a concept car that will have a large impact on future BMW vehicles'. As with the Z18, the Z22 project had actually begun in 1995, and was given an amazing list of goals that it needed to achieve. These included:

- the comfort and flexibility of a 528 tourer;
- automatic transmission;
- lightweight construction techniques;
- manufacture of at least 100 units per day;
- to achieve fuel consumption average figures of at least 39mpg (6ltr/100km);

- to meet stringent economic, environmental and recycling targets.

It is to BMW Technik's credit that all the above goals were achieved in a single vehicle, that could also carry five occupants in comfort – and their luggage needs, too. Externally conventional, except for its six headlamps and lack of mirrors, under the skin it was full of technical innovation, whilst its interior can only be described as 'space age'.

Covering the interior first, this included simplified, ultra-modern controls and screens. There was a rectangular-shaped, multi-purpose

The interior of the Z22 had simplified controls, including a specially shaped multi-function steering wheel. In place of the conventional gearshift was a central control known as the 'Man-Machine Interface' (MMI), which selected various functions and displayed the appropriate menus on a monitor screen located in the dash.

steering wheel that featured push-buttons to enable the driver to select a gear, use the light switch, cruise control or the horn, as well as set the foot pedals and head-up instrumentation display. Instead of the conventional gear shift there was a centrally mounted control console – BMW had labelled this MMI (Man-Machine Interface) – that selected various functions and displayed the appropriate menus on a dashboard-mounted monitor screen. It is also worth mentioning that BMW was later to employ this technology on the Z9 (*see* Chapter 13).

Another feature of the Z22 was its use of CFK (Carbon-Fibre-Reinforced Plastic) in its construction. This material, already widely used in the racing car and motorcycle field (and also in the existing Williams-BMW Formula 1 car), was extremely light and exceedingly strong. For example, the weight of carbon fibre is half that of steel and two-thirds that of aluminium.

An example of how the Z22 development will benefit series-production BMWs of the future, is to relate that CFK is being studied

and tested at the BMW research centre known as LITZ (Landshut Innovation and Technology Centre) in the town of the same name.

Countless Other Prototypes

The job of BMW Technik division is to create prototypes, and this it has done in abundance since its creation back in the mid-1980s. As is usual with prototypes, many remain just that; and of course there are the vehicles that never even make it into clay or metal and remain only drawings. So far we can account for the Z1, 2, 3, 4, 7, 8, 9, 11, 13, 14, 18, 21 and 22; but there was also talk of a Z12, similar to the Z8, but with a V12 engine from the 7 Series.

Only time will tell just how many Z types will actually reach series production, but the future looks interesting, to say the least. With the criticism levelled at BMW from certain sections of the world's motoring press, no doubt the company will be trying its very best to prove the doubters wrong.

12   The Z8 – High Class, High Cost

The Z8 was created to place the BMW sports car right up there with the likes of Ferrari, Lamborghini and Porsche. Not only this, it was also intended to pay homage to the legendary BMW 507 of the 1950s. Like the Z3, the Z8 enjoyed a show-business bonus when Pierce Brosnan used one in a James Bond film, *The World is not Enough*.

The Z8 on film duties whilst making The World is Not Enough.

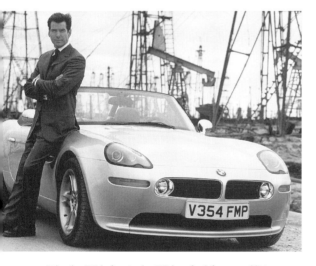

Like the Z3 before it, the Z8 benefited from a publicity viewpoint when one was used by Pierce Brosnan in the James Bond film The World is Not Enough.

BMW produced a postcard for the launch of the film The World is Not Enough.

Origins

In late 1997, the world was enchanted when BMW unveiled its Z07 concept car at the Tokyo Motor Show. This car was seen as the prototype successor to the legendary Albrecht

Goertz-designed 507 Roadster of the late 1950s. But even in the mid-1990s, rumours about a new, luxury, hyper-expensive BMW

The Z8 is by far the most expensive of the Z Series yet. Making its debut towards the end of 1999, it was based on the Z07 concept car that had first been seen at the 1997 Tokyo Motor Show. Both were designed by the young Dane, Henrik Fisker.

sports car had begun to surface. For example in *Car*, May 1995, there had been an artist's impression, although it must be said that it was totally different from the ultimate production Z8, or for that matter the prototype-only Z07. Then in the June 1996 issue of *Car* there was a four-page 'Newsdesk' story headlined 'Z3's Big Brother Breaks Cover – Aluminium-Bodied Coupé to become BMW's 400bhp, £90,000, Technical *Tour de Force*'.

In this article *Car* said that the Z8 was due 'to hit the streets in 1998' and that it was 'to be powered by the new 286bhp 4.4-litre V8, as well as a tweaked 6.0-litre version of the V12 5.6-litre 380bhp engine currently used in the 850csi Coupé.' *Car* went on to say:

> The spiritual successor to the 507 Roadster from the late 1950s, the Z8 will be sold in both Coupé

and Roadster guises, and is expected to be assembled in the experimental wing of BMW's Munich factory at a rate of 1,000 per year. If demand outstrips capacity, it is possible BMW will team up with a coachbuilder such as Karmann or Baur to continue production outside the factory.

The Reasons Why

Of course, the whole Z07/Z8 project was conceived as BMW's way of showing the world its ability to create a 'vehicle with technical ability and styling flair', rather than simply a means of generating profit. By the mid-1990s BMW chiefs had become very concerned that rival German manufacturers, such as Audi, had stolen a technological march on them by launching cars such as the aluminium-bodied A8.

During 1996 a senior BMW product planner had let slip that the Z8's prime role was that of 'image-lifter – a prestigious, highly visible product as a strategic answer to both the Mercedes Benz F1 racing programme and Audi's technical proficiency.' The same source even went as far as revealing 'We're going to lose money on this modern 507, and yet we feel it's an investment worth making.'

As further proof of just how BMW was worried, one may recall the bitter battle between VW (Audi's owners) and BMW over the ownership of the British prestige marque Rolls Royce – and that BMW were subsequently to return to F1 racing themselves in a deal with the Williams concern. This 'return', coming from the 2000 season onwards, was to such good effect that by the 2001 German Grand Prix, Ralf Schumacher had brought his Williams/BMW home to victory in front of the home crowd.

The Z8 Arrives

The final production version of the Z07/Z8 project made its public bow, at least in the 'metal', at the Frankfurt Motor Show in September 1999. Of the initial production batch of 1,500, just fifty examples were said to have been earmarked for the British market (this figure was later upped to seventy-five), and a right-hand-drive version was 'yet to be confirmed', a *BMW Car* magazine said in its September issue. However, though later it thought that an 'RHD version looks to be on the cards', it even then seemed to be wondering whether it would actually happen by saying: 'After all, surely neither the British nor the lucrative Japanese markets can be ignored?'

The Design

When the Z07 was built, it appeared in two guises: roadster and Coupé. However, it seems that the Z8 will remain a Roadster, at least for

the time being. But of course one can never tell, as the Z3 has shown with the independently conceived coupé variant.

For its styling cues, its young Danish designer, Henrik Fisker, obviously used the 507 as a starting point, or at least what he thought the 507 would have looked like had it been built forty years afterwards. The links between the two cars are obvious: unmissable elements include the trademark grille, along with the chromed air ducts and swage lines that were so much of the Z07 prototype's external lines.

However, there are major differences: for example, gone is the 1950s-style boot bulge behind the driver (along with the option of a

The Z8 (2000)	
Engine	Liquid-cooled, thirty-two-valve dohc V8
Displacement	4,941cc
Bore	94mm
Stroke	89mm
Transmission	Six-speed, manual
Doors	Two
Seats	Two
Chassis	Aluminium space-frame, monocoque
Bodywork	Aluminium
Drive	Rear wheel
Wheels	18in front and rear
Tyres	Front 245/45 R18
	Rear 275/40 R18
Dimensions	
Overall length	4,400mm (173in)
Overall width	1,830mm (72in)
Overall height	1,310mm (51.5in)
Wheelbase	n/a
Dry weight	1,585kg (3,495lb)
Max power	400bhp @ 6,600rpm
Max torque	369lb ft (500Nm) @ 3,800rpm
Top speed	Limited to 155mph (250km/h)
0–62mph (100km/h)	4.7sec

coupé variant). Instead, like the Z3, the Z8 is available with a hard top, making it practical to drive during the winter months.

The Cabin

The Z8's cabin is most definitely retro, but with a modern feel. Oddments' space is at a premium. There is a quartet of neat door pockets and two small recesses in the centre console, but the theoretically useful locking compartments behind the seats are taken up by a CD autochanger and the disc drive for the satellite navigation system. Although the cabin area is dominated by soft leather and high quality, body-coloured plastic, there is also an abundance of aluminium to give an added feeling of quality and light weight. For example, aluminium is used for all the switchgear. In fact, apart from the rim of the steering wheel, everything you touch – door handles, gear lever capping, heater and ventilation controls

The 507-style, multi-spoke steering wheel of the Z8 is best described as neo-classic. Like the rest of the car, it is beautifully executed.

The interior of the Z8 is truly stunning. A mere photograph does not capture the quality of the leather, aluminium or stainless-steel components that make up the Z8's cockpit. Ten-speaker hi-fi and sat-nav are standard.

(and the surrounding panels), column stalks and even the simple power window and mirror switch – all are cast from aluminium alloy. So are the 507-style multiple spokes for the neo-classic steering wheel. The substantial kickplates are manufactured in stainless steel.

In stark contrast to the old-fashioned starter button is the heavy, chip-loaded ignition key. The four centre-mounted circular instruments not only look classic, but even have white-on-black faces, that glow a reassuring soft orange when dusk falls. Power-operated, the seats are both supportive and comfortable. As the April 2000 issue of *Car* said: 'It's hard not to like this cab!'

The Engine

The M5 saloon is the donor of the Z8's quad-cam, thirty-two valve, V8 engine that displaces 4,941cc (94 × 89mm). Power output is 400bhp at 6,600rpm. This means that on dry, gripping tarmac, and with the DSC switched off, the Z8

The engine of the Z8 is the quad-cam, thirty-two valve, 4,941cc (94 × 89mm) V8 from BMW's M5. And as this photograph shows, it is mounted as far back as is possible in a front-mounted car, providing the perfect 50–50 weight distribution.

A real supercar, the mid-range punch of the V8-engined Z8 is truly breathtaking, with a 0–62mph (100km/h) figure of 4.7sec, the Z8 is BMW's quickest-accelerating car.

Cylinder block of the Z8's M5-sourced V8 engine.

The 4,941cc (94 × 89mm) V8 engine produces 400bhp at 6,600rpm.

can accelerate from 0–62mph (100km/h) in 4.7sec, leaving, as *Car* puts it, 'two long, Bridgestone signature stripes and a puff of smoke behind it'. The Z8 takes a mere 4.3sec from 50–70mph (80–112km/h) in fourth gear, and since the torque curve is almost flat all the way from 2,000 to 6,000rpm, also means strong fifth- and sixth-gear figures. In fact *Car* reckoned that 'nothing this side of a Lamborghini Diablo' beats the Z8 in terms of mid-range punch.

Redlined at 7,000rpm, the BMW V8 delivers 85 per cent of its maximum torque at an incredibly low 1,500rpm. Currently, the Z8 is only available in manual form, and it is unlikely that BMW will offer the much-improved SMG sequential 'box. But of course customer

demand, particularly in the States, may ultimately dictate otherwise.

Space-Frame Chassis

Claimed by BMW sources to be '30 per cent lighter than an equivalent steel component', the ultra-stiff aluminium space-frame chassis is an important factor in the Z8's character. Manufactured at BMW's Dingolfing plant, the key to its exceptional stiffness lies in its centre backbone structure, which is super-strong, flex-free, corrosion-resistant and, say BMW, easy to repair. This space-frame layout is combined with an infrastructure of extruded members and aluminium body panels.

Like certain other modern BMWs, aluminium is also used for the suspension. The

The styling of the Z8 may be retro, but under the aluminium skin everything is state-of-the-art technology. Several BMW insiders state that it's a dry run for the forthcoming Rolls-Royce venture, both in the quality of the bodywork and in the high-class engineering.

front axle is a variation of the spring/strut theme, whilst the rear suspension is of the integral four-link variety. Compact sub-frames act as cushions between the body and the moving components. Interestingly, no electronics are involved, or fancy kinematics, or ultra-sophisticated hardware, not even adjustable dampers. BMW suspension engineer Andreas Bovensiepan described it thus:

> The stiff body, the low centre of gravity, and even the perfect 50–50 weight distribution, are essential pre-conditions for good handling and roadholding qualities. Of course, we also devoted plenty of attention to tyres and brakes.

Braking

Much of the Z8's braking system is borrowed from the 750 luxury executive saloon, with huge 334mm discs at the front and 328mm discs at the rear, inner ventilated, but not cross-drilled. The 18in aluminium wheels are shod with run-flat (safe for 300 miles (500km)) Bridgestone Potenza tyres, 245/45 front and 275/40 rear. Their well-being is constantly monitored by an automatic tyre-pressure warning system.

No Extras List

Unlike rivals such as Porsche, BMW has redefined the 'total specification' statement. As with the Z8 it is absolutely true. The very

Massive 18in aluminium wheels are shod with runflat (safe for 300 miles) Bridgestone Potenza tyres.

comprehensive list of standard equipment includes satellite navigation, soft and hard tops, a car phone, stainless steel exhaust, airbags (front and side), Xenon headlamps, roll-over bars and lots more.

Costs

Even so, at £84,000 in the UK (2001), the Z8 was not cheap. But in its favour, as well as being a serious driver's car, the Z8 is certain to hold its value. With a total production run unlikely to exceed 8,000 examples and a controlled supply system, it should maintain strong residuals. It also substantially undercuts other upmarket convertibles such as the Mercedes-Benz 600SL (£96,370) and the Aston Martin DB7 Vantage (£99,950). It is rumoured that one day there is likely to be an even more awesome (and expensive) Z8 in the shape of the Z8M, featuring a body kit complete with rear spoiler, an uprated chassis, 20in wheels and a 530bhp 6-litre, twelve-cylinder engine. After driving the 'standard' Z8 I can only think that this will be an awesome missile indeed!

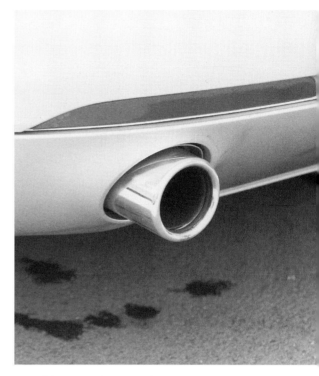

One of the two stainless-steel exhaust pipes that exit at the rear of the Z8; the whole system is in the same material.

Neon-strip rear lights are a world first in the automotive industry.

Super powerful Xenon headlights make night-driving a joy.

Road-Testing the Z8

Road-testing a BMW Z8 can be a daunting experience, especially if you have been loaned the vehicle, all £80,000 plus of it. Why? Well, to start with it is left-hand drive only, so in Great Britain the steering wheel is on the wrong side, and so too is the gear stick. And in addition the Z8 does look an expensive piece of kit compared to more mundane, mass-produced cars. Just looking at photographs simply does not do the V8-engined car full justice: you have to see it in the metal to appreciate just how impressive it really is.

For example, unlike the Z3 Series, the cabin is as impressive as the body style – in fact in many ways it is even better, with its superb bespoke feel. Several BMW insiders have openly admitted that in building the Z8, the company was doing a 'dry run' for its forthcoming BMW-powered Rolls Royce range of luxury saloons. Just looking at the Z8's dashboard is enough to make you excited – you simply cannot stop admiring it, and touching all that high-grade aluminium and stainless steel. In addition, simplicity is a major asset. A minimum of craftsman-like alloy switches are complemented by four classically retro, round-shaped dials in the centre of the dash. These are angled so that their position is not the problem one might have expected. The spoked 1950s-style steering wheel (except for the airbag equipment centre) is a talking point in itself. The 'S' button stands for 'Sport' mode and applies to the electronically controlled throttle, selecting the sport mode gives the driver a much sharper response to the pedal. To fire up the Z8 you simply insert and twist the key, and then press the separate black starter button: the 5-litre V8 (from the M5) will roar into life, with one of the greatest, most stirring sounds in the whole of the auto world. In its way it is just as fabulous as any TVR or Ferrari. Although it can be driven along in a sedate manner, the Z8 is seriously quick: put your foot down in the lower gears and you are pushed back in your seat in a manner few cars are capable of, the noise turning to a howl as you approach the rev limiter.

The six-speed gearbox takes a bit of getting used to, as it has a definite 'gate' movement. But if you do make a mistake, the manner of the Z8's power delivery covers up your error, thanks to its tremendous torque. For example, it is possible to pull away in third gear from a standstill if necessary. The M5-type 400bhp engine, with its double VANOS, variable valve timing, provides an even spread of power, and with an amazing 85 per cent of its torque available from a mere 1,500rpm, you do not have to work the six-speed gearbox hard.

Performance and Handling

Maybe this car has the performance I expected, but the handling and the ride are much better than I had imagined. As *Top Gear* said in its April 2000 issue: 'Traditional sports cars have choppy rides. This one doesn't. Traditional sports cars have handling that's fun but a bit unrefined. Not this one. And roadsters are as stiff as a wet envelope, flexing and shaking at every bump. Wrong again!'.

With its extra-long snout (longer than the Z3), you could be forgiven for thinking that the Z8's engine would be too far forward. But lift the bonnet and you see that the engine sits way back, giving the perfect front/rear weight distribution. This makes for a storming performance on twisty back roads. Maybe a mid-engined car would feel a little more nimble, but the Z8 gives the driver all the right tools – meaning that it is balanced, confident and chuckable as only a well sorted front-engined, rear-drive car can be.

There are various electronic driving aids, but even with the DSC (dynamic stability control) switched off, real provocation is needed to break traction. Added to this superb handling is the remarkably balanced ride. The secret to this is the Z8's body rigidity. This is one roadster where the word 'scuttleshake' does not enter the road tester's vocabulary. Quite simply, it feels as torsionally rigid as a car with a roof, allowing the chassis to play its full part in the enjoyment.

Manufactured in aluminium, the curvaceous body is built of big box sections running down the sills and the central tunnel and across at the screen and rear bulkhead areas, the whole assembly working together as a unit. Unlike the Z3's steering wheel, the one on the Z8 feels just the right size. The electrically operated seat adjustment allows a perfect driving position for all sizes of driver. Again, unlike the Z3, the electrically operated hood does not have to be assisted by part folding before the lowering process can begin. And there are no latches either, the double-skinned hood closing/opening with electrically operated catches (the windows need dropping slightly for this

continued overleaf

Road-Testing the Z8 *continued*

operation). The driver (not passenger) seems to sit further down in the Z8, so that wind buffeting of the upper part of the head does not take place except at very high speeds.

There are no optional extras for the Z8; this means that everything is standard, including CD autochange, satellite navigation, a cubby between the seats for a telephone, neon brake and indicator lighting (an industry first), roll-over hoops, stainless-steel exhaust (with twin tail-pipes) and 18in alloy wheels with newly developed run-flat Bridgestone tyres that allow you to go 300 miles (500km) at 50mph (80km/h) on a flat tyre (just as well because, like the Z3M, there is no spare wheel). There is nothing old fashioned about the safety features, as both the driver and passenger have front and side airbags; the radio is hidden away under a cover centrally, just forward of the gear lever, and there is an alarm/immobilizer.

Summary

Like its older, cheaper brother, the Z3, the press has not always been kind to the Z8. Most agree that it looks fabulous, but not all are impressed by its on-road performance. In the author's opinion some of this, like the criticism of the Z3, comes from the fact that BMW has built its Z Series to be used every day on public roads, not for rallying, racing or even track days. If you want a car for any of these pursuits, look elsewhere.

What the Z8 does, is provide awesome performance, certainly as much as any sane person would ever want or require on the public highways of the world; together with a beautifully crafted feel with scarcely a visible component from any other BMW. That of course, costs money, and at around £84,000 in the UK the Z8 is expensive. But with so few being made, residuals are likely to remain high. In the meantime you will be the owner of a very special piece of machinery, capable of bringing a smile to your face every time you drive it.

Press Reaction

Like the Z3, press reaction to the Z8 has been mixed, from the negative: 'Should have been the perfect home for the perfect engine. Left us strangely cold though. Simply too expensive' (*Autocar*); to 'The BMW Z8 is King of the Road, ruler of the overtaking lane, *boulevardier extraordinaire*. In a sector determined by style, speed and sportiness, BMW really does build the ultimate driving machine' (*Car*).

Summary

Like the mainstream Z3 Series, the Z8 does not please everyone. To start with, those looking for a raw-boned, 'real' sports car should look elsewhere, because what you get with the Z8 is a car that successfully (in the author's opinion) doubles as a cruiser and a speed machine, with a style, level of build quality and exclusiveness unmatched by virtually any other car on the road regardless of purchase price.

Like the Z3, the Z8 is not a track car, but for most potential owners this will not be a problem; living with the Z8 will be an exciting but painless experience. After all, who really wants to own a car with overhard suspension, potential unreliability and an engine that needs a service to run properly every other lamp post? Instead you get what you paid for – a superbly constructed, super-rapid, supercar.

13　The Z9 – The Future?

At the International Frankfurt Motor Show of 1999, BMW sprang a surprise by displaying a brand-new concept car. At what was the last Frankfurt exhibition of the twentieth century, here, said some observers, was a car to provide the technology, style and, hopefully, driving experience for the fast-upcoming new millennium.

Diesel Power

Besides its futuristic appearance, the other big talking point was its choice of powerplant type: thirty-two-valve turbo common-rail diesel V8, displaying 3,901cc (88 × 84mm). This produced 245bhp at 4,000rpm, but its biggest asset was the highly impressive torque figures of 413lb ft (560Nm) at 1,750–2,500rpm. This engine came from the 740d saloon and provided the fully working Z9 prototype with a maximum speed 'limited' to 156mph (251km/h). This was, of course, in line with German motor manufacturers' agreements over an industry-wide limit for that country's vehicles.

Dramatic Styling

Helping to make the Z9GT (Gran Turismo) – to give it its full title – such a show stopper was the dramatic styling, and this was thanks to Adrian van Hooydonk and Anne-Sophie Kramer, both of whom work in the department of BMW design chief Chris Bangle.

The long, curvaceous bonnet and relatively short rear provided the classic proportions for

Motive power of the Z9 is a thirty-two-valve V8 diesel with twin turbo-chargers. It is set well back to provide 50/50 balance, and thus aid handling.

a sporting coupé, hence the label GT. As one journalist put it, 'the detailing of the rear quarters recalls the tightened haunches of a big cat about to pounce'. Even so, it also incorporated enough traditional and current BMW styling cues to retain a family resemblance – so important to the Munich marque.

For example, the shape of the C-pillar off the window is pure BMW, whilst the cobby, flared wheel arches hint of models such as the Z3 roadster and current 3 Series saloon; and it was a clever combination of old and new that made a brilliant job of disguising the Z9's massive size. At 4,840mm (190.5in) long and almost 2,000mm (78.7in) wide, the concept coupé's footprint was virtually that of the existing 7 Series! A lack of height helped, of course, with the Z9 being much lower than the 7 Series, at nearly 1,350mm (53.1in). The wheelbase was 3,100mm (122in), which allowed room for four adults.

Dual Function Doors

A unique feature of the Z9 was its dual-function doors. The huge Mercedes-Benz 300SL-type butterfly wings have been a guaranteed crowd-puller since the 1950s, but BMW engineers took the concept a stage further; and they did it very cleverly. Within the frame of each vast, top-hinged door was a second, conventionally hinged door. If the car was parked too close to a wall for the gull-wing door to be safely opened, the conventional

The Z9 Gran Turismo concept car was the star of the 1999 Frankfurt Motor Show. Gull-wing doors are always a crowd puller. But will a production version of the Z9 ever reach the showrooms?

door allowed access to the front seats. Thus the Z9 could be moved to a more suitable point of exit for the rear passengers to alight. Following this procedure it was simply a case of, latch a few latches and press the remote button on the key fob, and the gull-wing doors were able to open smoothly and automatically to give sufficient access for the rear seat passengers. If only the driver and front seat passenger were entering, the wings stayed firmly shut and the two 'ordinary' doors opened to let them in. A remote-control electronic key activated the entry system, with two more presses of the button opening the conventional doors integrated within the panel work. The same key also unlocked the on-board electronic system. Inserted into a slot in the central console, the key released a cover over the flat screen of the Z9's computer.

Electronic Controls

The central control unit was in the position normally occupied by the gear lever, and could be operated by driver or passenger alike. It comprised a single button that could be turned or pressed, and which had four positions, for gears, comfort, communication and audio.

Transmission

The five-speed automatic transmission with Steptronic control ensured that the great power and torque produced by the engine was transmitted to the rear wheels with the very minimum of fuss or energy on the part of the driver. And to ensure that sufficient grip was available, the Z9 was shod with huge racing specification tyres on wheels larger than any of the existing BMW production line. At the front these had a diameter of 20in, whilst the rears were even bigger, at 21in. The rubber, courtesy of Dunlop, was 245/45 at the front, and a massive 285/40 at the rear.

Innovative Dashboard

The Z9's dashboard was developed under the leadership of the Advanced Design Department's boss Thomas Plath, and stunned many show-goers by having only two (yes, just two!) switches: one for the starter and the other for the lights. Every other function is controlled from the 220mm (8in) square computer screen in the dashboard, which is revealed when the ignition 'key' transponder is inserted. As already described, a rotary control on the centre console, in the location normally occupied by the gear lever, allows both the driver and the front passenger to select the appropriate menu, which is then displayed on the screen. So that, although the number of external controls is minimal, the number of functions via the computer is almost endless, from stiffening the rear damper settings to ringing your secretary to rearrange a business engagement.

Conventional Touches

If the computer technology is state of the art, at least BMW's Z9 engineering team decided to retain a conventional steering wheel. This is an attractive two-spoke affair, with press buttons for the Steptronic gear change. There is a gear lever, too, even if it is only a tiny 'stick' hidden away on the steering column, retained simply to select forward or reverse. The speedometer and tachometer were taken from the Z8, and were housed in hooded binnacles. The clock (also from the Z8) attempts to balance them visually on the passenger's side – but their large round dials seem almost at odds with the otherwise largely space-ship-like interior.

Chassis and Bodywork

The Z9 concept car was built around an aluminium space-frame, the technology being shared with the Z8 Roadster, and its outer skin panels manufactured from carbon fibre. This

The Z9 Concept Car (1999)

Engine	V8, thirty-two-valve diesel, twin turbochargers; liquid-cooled
Displacement	3,901cc
Bore	84mm
Stroke	88mm
Transmission	Five-speed automatic gearbox, with Steptronic control system on steering wheel
Doors	Gull-wing, with a second conventionally hinged door
Seats	Four
Chassis	Aluminium space-frame
Bodywork	Carbon-fibre reinforced synthetic materials
Drive	Rear wheel
Wheels	Front 20in
	Rear 21in
Tyres	Front 245/45 × 20
	Rear 285/40 × 21
Dimensions	
Overall length	4,840mm (190.5in)
Overall width	2,000mm (78.7in)
Overall height	1,350mm (53.1in)
Wheelbase	3,100mm (122in)
Dry weight	n/a
Max power	245bhp @ 4,000rpm
Max torque	413lb ft @ 1,750–2,500rpm
Top speed	Limited to 155mph (251km/h)
0–62mph	n/a

The Z9 was a very innovative car, and as such represented the very latest thinking of BMW's design team. Even if it is not built as a production car, several of its design features are likely to be incorporated in future vehicles.

Besides the Coupé, BMW also built this Roadster version in 2000; it was even prettier than its older brother.

weight-saving is expensive, but it is evident that it will be more widely used by BMW in the future. Officially, BMW claim that its space-frame construction is 'much cheaper than a conventional monocoque for a limited-volume vehicle'. In the longer term, the Munich marque envisages an increase in what it calls 'niche models', and a decrease in today's broad model ranges: so space-frame technology is very likely to play an ever-increasing role in the company's future designs.

The Future?

Although it is highly unlikely that a production version of the Z9 concept car will be offered for sale, it has many aspects that make it far more than the typical motor show special. And undoubtedly, much of the technology will find its way – possibly sooner than you would think – into the forthcoming BMW cars. Fitting a diesel engine also points to the future, where fuel economy and the growing sophistication of the diesel power unit may well see it eventually overtake the conventional petrol engine

as the Munich car maker's first choice. But whatever happens, working prototypes such as the Z9 mean that BMW is not resting on its laurels; instead, the German auto giant is not just looking for revolutionary improvements, but radical advances, too.

The interior of the Z9 Roadster (BMW called it a 'convertible'): ultra modern, with satellite navigation and every luxury.

14   The Z4 – A Fresh Style

In the summer of 2002, BMW released the first official pictures of the new Z4 Roadster. The car was shown at the Paris Motor Show in September the same year, and was the long-forecast replacement for the Z3. It was scheduled to go on sale in the UK in the summer of 2003, though the American market would receive its first supplies towards the end of 2002. But how will sales compare with the outgoing Z3 Series?

A Controversial Styling Job

The first thing that anyone notices about a new car – in contrast to an updated one – is its styling, and with the Z4, this was even more controversial than the love-it-or-hate-it Z3M Coupé. The work of the American Chris Bangle, head of Design Development for BMW, the Z4 has already divided opinions between

The Z4 is ultra modern, where its forerunner the Z3 was unashamedly retro. At first it will be available with either the 2.5- or the 3-litre six-cylinder. The Z4's styling is the work of American designer Chris Bangle, but will it prove a commercial success?

As with the Z3, Chris Bangle's Z4, with its long nose and short tail, looks best from the front. The styling works well from this angle.

The rear half of the Z4 is definitely its weakest point. Even so, the BMW badge, strong performance and excellent ergonomics have produced a car that only the Porsche Boxster can better in its price range.

those who love it, and those who hate it more violently than virtually any previous BMW. Definitely in the 'love it' camp is *BMW Car* editor Bob Harper, who in the August 2002 issue said: 'Personally I think it's a cracking design, as modern and up to date as the Z3 was retro!' But even Harper's magazine had to agree that: 'The styling might not be everyone's cup of tea, however.'

Then there was *Auto Express* reader David Mercer, who was full of praise for the new car's style. But Mercer's opinions were quickly rubbished by another reader, R. Rouse, who in *Auto Express* 'Car of the Year Awards' issue had this to say:

I'm sorry David Mercer, but you're definitely in the minority with your view about the BMW Z4. The company has let Chris Bangle loose with the crayons again, and I think he's produced yet another mess. You have to wonder if he's a closet pyromaniac, with his obsession for flames! Judging by the flanks on the sides of the new two-seater, I can only assume that American flames are different to English ones, and must resemble large dents.

BMW Car refers to that styling as 'a complex amalgam of straight edges, convex and concave surfaces, and gentle curves – the infamous "flame surfacing" design from the X Coupé, and to a lesser extent the CSI concept, can clearly be seen.'

In a straw poll the author carried out between the styling of the 2002 Z3 3.0 and its replacement the Z4, the Z3 came out top by at least three to one – and to a larger degree by existing Z3 owners. And those styling questions *included* the interior, a particular dislike of the latter being the squared-off roll-over bars.

However, whatever you think of its styling merits, the Z4 has much to commend it technically and in its expected on-road abilities.

At the time this book was being written, it had not been possible to drive the new roadster. But BMW stated that the Z4 '…will be available with two six-cylinder engines'. The 3.0-litre put out 231bhp and had a maximum speed of 155mph (250km/h), whilst the 2.5 unit offered 192bhp and a speed of 146mph

The Z4 went on sale in the USA towards the end of 2002 and in Britain in June 2003.

(235km/h). The Z4 3.0 features a new, six-speed manual gearbox. SSG, BMW's sequential manual gearbox, will be available as an option on both engine sizes. This second-generation system features a modified six-speed transmission, and enables the driver to make instant gear changes via paddles on the steering wheel or with the conventional gear selector lever. The 2.5 model uses a five-speed manual, with a six-speed SSG as an option.

Chris Bangle

BMW's current head of Design Development, Christopher Edward Bangle, was born on 14 October 1956 at Ravenna, Ohio, USA. After attending primary school, he went to the Wausau West High School, Wisconsin from 1972 until 1975. Later that year, just turned nineteen years of age, he took up Liberal Arts Studies at the University of Wisconsin.

In 1977 Chris Bangle moved to the Art Centre College of Design, Pasadena, where he subsequently gained his Batchelor of Science Degree with Honours in 1981.

During 1978 Chris Bangle had been appointed assistant designer at Hartkopf Associates. Then in 1981 he joined the German company, Adam Opel AG, in their Interior Design Department, becoming its Deputy Head of Interior Design in 1983, a post he held up to 1985.

In 1985 he joined the Italian Fiat organization, in the company's automobile division, Fiat Centro *Stile* (style). Up to the end of 1990 he was Head of Exterior Studies; from then until December 1991 he headed the Exterior Design house of Centro Stile. From January until September 1992 he held the position of Director of Fiat Centro Stile/Design. He is generally credited, among other designs, with that of the Fiat Coupé, launched in the mid-1990s.

On 1 October 1992, Chris Bangle was appointed Head of Design Development at BMW AG, Munich. For the first few years of his reign Chris Bangle seemed content to maintain the status quo; however, since the boardroom shake-up that saw the removal of Pischetsrieder and Reitzle, more radical styling, generally accredited to Bangle, has begun to appear, notably the latest 7 Series, the Compact, and most recently the Z4. With the latter, it seems that the American is taking BMW away from the retro style of the Z3/Z8 models and on to a more modern, futuristic style.

The Z4 3.0i (2003)	
Engine	Liquid-cooled, dohc, straight six with four valves per cylinder, double VANOS and fuel injection
Bore and stroke	84 × 89.6mm
Displacement	2,979cc
Compression ratio	10.2:1
Max power	231bhp at 5,900rpm
Engine management	MS45
Clutch	Dry
Gearbox	Six-speed
Front suspension	Single-joint spring-strut axle with displaced caster; small positive steering roll radius; compensation of transverse forces; anti-dive
Rear suspension	Independent, centrally guided axle, separate springs and damper; anti-squat and anti-dive
Front brakes	300mm vented discs with ABS
Rear brakes	294mm vented discs with ABS
Steering	Electric power steering (EPS)
Wheels	8J × 17 cast aluminium
Tyres	225/45 R-17 91W
Fuel tank	55ltr (12gal)
Dry weight	1,365kg (3,010lb)
Wheelbase	2,495mm (98in)
Acceleration	0–62mph (0–100km/h) 5.9sec
Max speed	155mph (250km/h)

After all the criticism from the press, if not from the customer, of the Z3's on-the-road abilities, the BMW engineering team made this a priority, with particular attention to agility and handling. It featured a modified floorpan and rear axle from the very latest 3 Series, which should ensure that it is equally suited to cross country, road work or track-day antics. And in keeping with the Z4's sporting focus, it will feature DDC ('dynamic drive control'), activated by pressing the 'sport' button on the central console. DDC (now in its third series) re-maps the engine management system to deliver a more sporting response to inputs from the accelerator pedal, whilst also providing a change in the steering weight to deliver a more direct feel.

Another definite improvement over the out-going Z3 Series is the boot – at 260ltr (57gal), it is a full 95ltr (9.1cu ft) up on the older car. The BMW publicity machine makes a big play of '…enough space for two golf bags', and indeed, whatever it holds, the extra space will be of considerable benefit for a whole series of individual needs.

Actually, except for the new styling and improved chassis, the 50–50 front/rear weight distribution, the rear-wheel drive, two-seat road-ster layout, the long wheelbase with short over-hangs, wide track, long bonnet and short rear section, and a low centre of gravity, are all features to be found on the outgoing Z3. Even so, the Z4 is very much, as BMW says, 'an all-new car'.

At present there is no word as to whether the aforementioned six-cylinder engine will feature BMW's revolutionary Valvetronic cylinder heads (at the time of writing only to be found on the new British-made 1.8- and 2.0-litre four-cylinder engines), but with BMW's love of continual improvement to its

---

The Z4 2.5i (2003)

Engine	Liquid-cooled, dohc, straight six with four valves per cylinder, double VANOS and fuel injection
Bore and stroke	84 × 75mm
Displacement	2,494cc
Compression ratio	10.5:1
Max power	192bhp at 6,000rpm
Engine management	MS45
Clutch	Dry
Gearbox	Five-speed
Front suspension	Single-joint spring-strut axle with displaced caster; small positive steering roll radius; compensation of transverse forces; anti-dive
Rear suspension	Independent, centrally guided axle, separate springs and damper; anti-squat and anti-dive
Front brakes	286mm vented discs
Rear brakes	280mm vented discs
Steering	Electric power steering (EPS)
Wheels	7J × 16 cast aluminium
Tyres	225/50 R-16 92V
Fuel tank	55ltr (12gal)
Dry weight	1,335kg (2,944lb)
Wheelbase	2,495mm (98in)
Acceleration	0–62mph (0–100km/h) 7sec
Max speed	146mph (235km/h)

---

power units, this would not be a surprise. Although it has to be said in the case of the 2.8 and 3.0 Z3 units, power was never a failing.

The Z4 Interior

The interior of the Z4 is, like the outside, a complete change from the retro-styled Z3. And, it has to be said, very modern. The Z4 will be available with the typical extensive BMW options list, but unlike the Z3, this will now include a satellite navigation system that retracts fully into the instrument panel. Other notable options include a car telephone, and state-of-the-art hi-fi equipment. Standard features include leather upholstery and a leather steering wheel, the latter based on the one found in the Z8 (and also of a smaller diameter than the Z3 type), but with solid spokes, rather than the Z8's

split ones – and as *BMW Car* said, 'looks all the better for it'. And at first glance the cabin's appearance has a brighter feel to it than the rather sombre Z3's. The Z4's cabin also promises to be roomier than the Z3 – although it has to be said that I've never been uncomfortable in a Z3.

Other standard features on the Z4 include a roll-over safety system, and a Z-folding, fully automatic roof retraction system with a heated glass rear window. Again, the latter is a definite improvement over the Z3's plastic component. Previously if one wanted a heated glass rear window it was only possible by purchasing either the expensive hardtop, or the M Coupé as regards the Z3 Series.

However, I for one, still question whether it wouldn't have been better for sales to have used styling more akin to the Z3, but with the undoubted technical and chassis improvements.

Using the floor plan and rear axle from the very latest 3 Series saloon, the on-road abilities should be significantly superior to its older brother, the Z3.

Did BMW carry out its own poll, I wonder? Even *BMW Car* ended its Z4 launch article by admitting: 'The styling might not be everyone's cup of tea.'

The other area of doubt concerning the Z4 is that at present there is no mention of either a cheaper four-cylinder model, or a barnstorming M variant. And there seems small likelihood of a Z4 coupé. So unless BMW has plans for a wider range than the two sixes on offer at present, sales figures are unlikely to get anywhere near those of the Z3.

But maybe the answer to just how BMW will make up this expected shortfall in Z4 sales is to be found in the 31 July 2002 issue of the *Autocar*. And as *Autocar* points out, the following are the reasons why BMW needs to address the problem:

> Munich shifted 297,087 Z3s in its six years on sale, but increased competition and a price hike means the Z4 is unlikely to reap that success …Around 35,000 Z2 (*Autocar's* expected budget-priced BMW Roadster) sales a year would compensate –

as well as bolster BMW's growth from 600,000 in 1995, to 900,000 cars last year (2001).

The essence of *Autocar's* story was that BMW is secretly developing a 'back-to-basics' sports car to give the top-selling Mazda MX-5 a roasting in the showroom. *Autocar* goes on to say: 'Code-named E82/2 but set to carry the name Z2 into production – in keeping with Munich's revised badging policy – the junior Roadster will be pitched at young enthusiasts on a budget.' *Autocar* forecast that in the UK, 'The car is expected to cost well under £20,000.'

Autocar also reported that one BMW insider had revealed that: 'BMW board members are evenly split between the Z2 and a more conventional four-seat 1 series cabriolet, previewed by the CSI at the Geneva Show earlier this year (2002).'

Also, as the *Autocar* computer-generated image revealed, Z2's styling was likely to be heavily influenced by the Z4's 'modern look'.

All this very much goes to prove that in the new Z4 and the likely Z2, the retro style of the

There is no doubting that the Z4's cabin is, like the rest of the car, much more modern than the Z3. The steering wheel is based on the Z8 and is of a smaller diameter than the Z3, which is no bad thing.

previous generation of Z cars – the outgoing Z3 and limited volume supercar Z8 – has been consigned to the history books.

So this gets back to one last question: why – and strangely, as if by a quirk of fate, the answer may lie in the launch of the revised 'Porsche Boxster'. This is how the August 2002 issue of *Car* reported the event: 'If it ain't broke …an oh-so-subtle round of tweaks leaves the Boxster pretty much where it always was: right at the top of the Roadster pile'. Reporter Mike Duff went on the say:

Not with a bang, but with a tinker, so one could categorize another round of very mild revisions just delivered to the Porsche Boxster. Rather like a previous, extremely mild spec-tweaking session back in 1999. And, as with three years ago, there hasn't been a whole lot of change. Somehow I managed to resist the temptation to use cut-and-paste function from my story on the last Boxster revisions. I really have no problem with Porsche spending thousands of pounds to fly me and most of the motoring hack-pack to Italy to demonstrate a substantially identical car. Indeed, if they want to do it more often, I'll happily go along every time and faithfully report findings. But for here and now, the most important question is probably why the Boxster is still number one.

So now we return to the Z4 (and possibly the Z2) and the Z3/Z8 Series.

The Z3 came out at around the same time as the Boxster (and also the Mercedes SLK). Unlike Porsche and Mercedes, BMW chose the retro path – which, of course, made the car look from an earlier generation. This was something their German rivals didn't attempt. Now it all depends if you like the word 'classic' or not. Personally, I love the styling of the Z3. I also love the SLK, and I love that of the Boxster. And here comes the crunch – at the present time I haven't fallen in love with the Z4. Maybe, just maybe it may grow on me. I have to concede, however, that it's modern. Will modern and efficient and its improved chassis prove enough for the Z4 to pull it off? Only time will tell – and a drive, of course.

Testing the Z4: The Car Described

The first test of the new Z4, reported by *Autocar* in their 9 October 2002 issue, showed just how controversial the Z3's replacement is. Editor Steve Fowler began by saying 'style is a very personal thing', and went on to say:

Take BMW's new Z4. I reckon it's a cracker, and I take back everything I ever said about its designer Chris Bangle, after the launch of the 7 Series.

But there's a distinctly furrowed look on Steve Sutcliffe's brow. He's been spending time in the Z4, and is less convinced by its beauty.

As for the test itself, Sutcliffe's view was that in many ways it was a considerable improvement over the car it replaced, but was still 'not a true sports car'. However, even *Autocar's* experienced tester didn't really seem sure of what he was saying, as elsewhere in the test he commented: 'The basic message about the Z4 is unequivocal: this time it's a serious sports car, not a wash-out like before.' And he is also quoted as saying: 'The way the Z4 controls the movements of its body at high speed over rough roads is more than impressive'.

Other features Sutcliffe praised included the brakes, the engine (the car tested had the 3 litre, 231bhp straight six), the cabin ('a minor miracle'), the driving position, gearbox, torque and response ('better than a Boxster's low down'); he observed that above 4,000rpm, the engine 'unashamedly replicates that of a flat six at full chat'. But in the end, Sutcliffe considered that the jury was still out on the styling, and clearly voiced his own opinion on the matter: 'Please, don't try to convince me it's a car with the same emotional pull, the same clarity of response as a Boxster.' Another area of contention was the roof. Sutcliffe again:

> So what, no big deal, I hear you say? Well, fair enough; but just remember, the 3.0-litre Z4 will likely be priced within a grand of a Porsche Boxster when it goes on sale next spring – and yet the Boxster has a fully electric hood. Which will effectively (if the optional electric hood is specified) make the Z4 more expensive than its arch rival in the showroom.

It is worth pointing out that the Z3 in six-cylinder guise came with an electric roof as standard in the UK. Nevertheless, even the *Autocar* tester found much of the Z4 to his liking. The following in-depth analysis of its design reveals why.

Almost, an All-new Car

Technically, the Z4 is almost an all-new car, if one discounts the fact that the engine ranges – at launch 2.5 and 2.0-litre straight sixes, and from spring 2003, 2.2 straight six – are largely those found in other cars in BMW's vast range. Also the Z4 features a modified version of the current 3 Series chassis, with that car's much acclaimed multi-link rear suspension, rather than the ancient semi-trailing arm rear end from the 3 Series of two generations, removed from the outgoing Z3.

Otherwise virtually everything that moves on the Z4 is new, as is the entire styling exercise. But although the basic platform may be from the 3 Series, the wheelbase, measuring 2,495mm (98.2in), is considerably shorter, whilst the track is significantly wider at each end. All the spring, damper and bush rates are bespoke. So in reality, only 3 Series' basics remain.

Suspension

Weight distribution on the two axles is an ideal 50:50, providing great balance, and of course the Z4, like all current BMWs, is rear-wheel drive. The wide track relative to the body, as well as the anti-roll bars at both front and rear, enhance driving stability, providing minimum shift in dynamic wheel loads. This effect is assisted further by the unsprung masses being kept to a minimum, the share of light alloys employed on the suspension now amounting to some 60kg (130lb), or approximately 4 per cent of the car's overall weight.

In terms of its design and configuration, the front axle is a spring-strut structure with forged aluminium track-control arms, twin-sleeve gas-pressure spring struts, rack-and-pinion steering and anti-roll bar. The central-arm rear axle with dual-sleeve gas-pressure dampers and anti-roll bar benefits from the optimum combination of the rear axle sub-frame and the body, the engineering team commenting 'the firm connection of these two units ensuring very safe handling and preventing any uncontrolled steering behaviour'. BMW has also provided for a more sporting performance on the road, namely an optional M Technic sports suspension package for the Z4: this lowers the entire body by 15mm (0.6in).

Bodyshell

After the criticism received from the European press and hard-driving enthusiasts in respect of the Z3's bodyshell (except for the M coupé, and to a lesser extent the fitment of a hard top), the Z4's development centred around providing improved torsional stiffness to its body structure. Compared with the Z3's figure of 5,600Nm/degree, the Z4's torsional stiffness figure of 14,500Nm/degree was more than twice as stiff and stable in its body structure. BMW went so far as to claim:

> Never before has a convertible or Roadster offered this kind of body stiffness, providing a perfect solution to the conflict of interests between saloon-like smoothness and vibration control, on the one hand, and dynamic, sporting suspension on the other.

To achieve this level of stiffness and stability, the Z4's bodyshell incorporates a Y-structure carrier design, the engine supports splitting up in front of the bulkhead into one side-sill and one propeller shaft section on each side. Additional reinforcement bars and thrust plates in the underfloor, on the spring strut domes and in the windscreen frame help to ensure the high-level torsional stiffness – and because of this the Z4 does not, in BMW's opinion, 'require any further features such as a vibration damper.'

The Z4 has what the BMW engineering team describes as a 'weight-optimized concept', including an aluminium engine compartment lid (bonnet), rollbars integrated in the basic body structure, and high-strength steel panels used wherever appropriate. Application of the most advanced production methods, such as inner high-pressure moulding, allows design- and weight-optimized configuration of the windscreen frame without any welding flanges, which would ultimately weaken the entire structure.

BMW claims that the advantage of the above technology is a low weight, of 1,260kg (2,778lb) overall (unladen weight) on the Z4 2.5, ensuring an excellent power-to-weight ratio. Weighing 1,290kg (2,844lb), the 3-litre version is some 25kg (55lb) lighter than the outgoing Z3 3-litre model – despite larger exterior dimensions, larger wheels and a six-speed gearbox.

Passive Safety

The Z4's ultra-stiff bodyshell, and the use of high-strength steel wherever possible, means that the newcomer has a high standard of passive safety for both the driver and passenger. The A-pillars in the Z4 design form a rollbar in front for the occupants, extra-strong steel tubes anchored in the A-pillar by a massive steel structure reinforcing both pillars and the roof frame.

Two steel rollbars behind the seats of the Z4 are welded to the body cross-member in the bulkhead; these are able to withstand high loads, and so are integrated ideally into the body structure. Crash-optimized foot-support panels help prevent any intrusion into the passenger compartment, which could potentially endanger the occupants. Long deformation elements in the steel shell structure are welded on to the front chassis legs, connected in turn to the bumper system; this ensures that in minor collisions the welded body structure will remain free of damage, thus keeping repair costs to a minimum.

The Z4 has four airbags as standard, the driver's in the hub of the steering wheel, the passenger bag fitted out of sight in the instrument panel; finally, side airbags are integrated within the doors.

Advanced Safety Electronics

By introducing ASE ('advanced safety electronics'), BMW is once again setting the standard in safety technology. ASE is a networked airbag control system that for the first time uses lightwave conductors. Like the ISIS network in the new 7 Series, ASE is structured as a satellite system where the satellites ensure individual, optimum activation of the individual airbags as required. Each module measures and calculates impacts by itself, responds individually on demand, and supervises (just as it is supervised by) all the other modules.

The decision as to when a component is activated, and in what way, thus no longer depends exclusively on the central control unit. Rather, the decision is taken at the point where the airbag is actually required. Both the central control module and the satellites feature accelerometers for this purpose. By combining the satellite concept with lightwave technology, the system reliably detects the specific nature of each collision and guarantees activation of the appropriate airbags promptly. A further feature integrated into the system is a battery connection monitor: this reliably disconnects the safety battery terminal, thus stopping the fuel supply, opening the central locking, and switching on the hazard warning flashers when required.

The system also allows full integration of a child seat, in which case the passenger airbag has to be deactivated for safety reasons. This is achieved by an 'airbag off' switch, together with a warning light in the central console.

Depending upon the country of sale, the Z4 comes as standard with the child seats or available from BMW as dealer-fit accessories.

Runflat Tyres

Yet another indication of how seriously the Z4 design team took the safety issue is that BMW's new roadster comes as standard with puncture-proof tyres (17in 3ltr, 16in 2.5ltr).

In their design and structure, these self-bearing tyres incorporate reinforced sidewalls with additional inserts; they employ temperature-resistant rubber compounds that prevent the tyres from giving way when they have no pressure inside, thus allowing the driver to continue for a certain distance after experiencing a puncture. Driving at a speed of not more than 50mph (80km/h), the driver of a Z4 can cover up to 90 miles (150km) without risk even when one or more tyres are flat. This will normally allow him to reach a service station without having to stop at a dangerous location, or risk changing the wheel on, say, a motorway hard shoulder.

The driver is informed of any loss of pressure in good time by a tyre-pressure monitor – also fitted as standard – that gives a visual signal. Basically, this works on the principle that any loss of air pressure will change the roll radius of the tyre and, as a result, its circumference too. This, in turn, will increase the tyre's speed of rotation. Measuring tyre speed by means of the sensors in the four-channel ABS brake system, the tyre-pressure monitor compares the wheels diagonally with one another, determining their average speed and recognizing any loss of pressure. This information is provided by the tyre-pressure monitor after a relatively short distance, usually within 1–3min and at speeds of more than 9mph (15km/h). A further advantage is that, provided no puncture has been inflicted, such an early warning also enables the driver to inflate the tyres before expensive tyre damage is sustained. Statistically up to 80 per cent of all tyre damage is the result of inadequate air pressure – which the Z4 driver can now avoid with the help of this system.

Under normal driving conditions, runflat tyres offer the same level of performance as all tyres recommended and supplied by BMW. Furthermore, being fully compatible with the standard wheel/tyre system, runflat may be replaced, if necessary, by a conventional, standard tyre.

The Z4 Design, Development and Production Processes

Production

Like its predecessor the Z3, the Z4 is built exclusively for the world market at BMW's American Spartanburg facilities. At the time of writing (spring 2003) the workforce there totalled 4,000; currently production centres on the X5 (introduced in 1999) and the new Z4. Commenting on the Z4's production, Dr Helmut Leube, plant manager and president of BMW's Spartanburg operation had this to say:

> In starting production of the Z4, our associates (employees) successfully mastered the challenge of introducing the new Roadster on pre-series production while continuing production of the Z3 and X5. Then production was ramped up to the planned volume within about three months.

A brief look at the past demonstrates the huge progress made in this area, since a decade ago the actual process of ramping up a new model would have taken two to three times as long.

The Development Process

The exceptionally short and therefore demanding schedule with the Z4 was only possible because of the integration at an early stage of all departments at the US plant in the 'product creation process', as BMW calls it: that of the entire cycle of design, construction and series development. Key specialists in logistics, body construction, paint application, assembly, quality control and component procurement were integrated for this purpose in the development process at BMW's R&I (Research and Innovation) centre in Munich. Some 150 personnel from Spartanburg went to Germany in order to gain experience and knowledge in prototype construction, at the same time contributing their own knowledge. And last but not least, the most advanced methods of communication, such as an internet-based information platform, for everyone involved, and the use of tools and virtual technologies ensuring a consistent flow of data, ensured that transmission of information between the development division and the Spartanburg plant was smooth and efficient.

Back at Spartanburg, by concentrating all production technologies under one roof, BMW has an extremely efficient structure for the fast and smooth flow of data, components and expertise between sections, including the paintshop, bodyshop, assembly area, logistics and quality control (BMW calls the latter 'quality assurance').

Bodyshop

Constructing the precise and sophisticated bodyshell of the Z4 with several hundred components calls for particular expertise in the joining and welding processes, as well as the use of materials. Welding spots and connection seams have to be applied with the utmost precision. The Spartanburg bodyshop building the Z4 has a high degree of automation (around 95 per cent), using some 100 industrial robots for welding, transportation and quality control. Masterminded and controlled by body construction specialists, these processes ensure that the all-important BMW name for quality is maintained.

To prepare the bodyshop – which covers an area of more than 19,000sq m (200,000sq ft) for production of the Z4 – it was necessary to install quickly the plant technology and equipment needed, the engineering team using virtual planning tools in the advance phase to precisely simulate and test all processes, ensuring optimum working conditions and utilizing the space available to the maximum efficiency. With the help of computer software programs in the planning process, the engineers were able to quickly program the industrial robots and install the required plant technology within a period of only three months. As a result, the first prototypes were constructed in the bodyshop itself, using series production tools a number of months before production as such was scheduled to commence.

The Spartanburg projects manager Yimin Zhang commented:

The Z4 is a very complex car. Compared to its predecessor, this Roadster has far more parts and components, with more welding spots, and that makes processes more complicated. A further point is that the Z4 features an aluminium engine compartment lid (bonnet) that serves to reduce the overall weight of the body, optimizing front-to-rear weight distribution and, ultimately, improving the car's dynamics and fuel economy.

Paintwork

A good paint finish is all-important, and BMW has an excellent reputation in this respect. Paint is applied with the most advanced technology in the field, providing, in the words of the company: 'Supreme paint quality and a saving of resources at the same time'. Indeed, the Spartanburg factory was the first car-production facility in the USA to use water-based paint all the way from the primer to the basic paint providing the colour desired, with BMW commenting: 'In this way ensuring a high level of sustainability and helping preserve resources'.

In all, the Z4, like every current BMW, receives four layers of paint: the primer, filler, basic paint, and clear topcoat. The basic layer gives the car its colour, the clear topcoat adds the brilliant look and ensures lasting protection against the environment.

The first step in applying the paint is to clean the body of the car, removing grease and then applying a thin layer of zinc phosphate, forming the foundation for the four layers of paint to follow. The first layer is applied in a cathodic dip bath, the electrostatic charge effect being used in the bath to spread out the paint consistently on the entire surface of the car. This is followed by the filler, dried, like all other layers, in the furnace. And when the basic coating and the top coat are applied, then finally the body takes on its actual colour as lustre.

To ensure that as much of the topcoat as possible is sprayed on to the car and not elsewhere, the Spartanburg paintshop again uses the electrostatic charge effect. Charged electrically and atomized into extremely fine particles, the paint coming out of the spray nozzles is drawn onto the body, connected to earth like a magnet. Ultra-fine filters in the air-supply system, excess pressure in the paint application booths, air showers at the entrances, and fluff-free suits worn by employees, ensure that no dust or impurities are able to reach the paint.

Finally, the painted bodyshells are checked in specially illuminated test areas and have to be approved by the trained eye of experienced paintwork specialists for perfect quality, before moving on to the Assembly Division.

Assembly

Hi-tech machines and highly qualified staff work hand-in-hand on the assembly area. This is where the engine, transmission, axles, windows, panels and all attachments and equipment options ordered by the customer are fitted into the fully painted body to provide a tailor-made finish.

Many thousands of component parts going into a Z4 are assembled in advance to provide complete modules ready for installation – for example, the drivetrain with the engine, transmission front axle, as well as the doors and bumpers, which are then supplied to the assembly line.

The cockpit module is particularly complex, being made up, as it is, of the instrument panel, instrument panel support, airbag/s, steering column and air conditioning. This is pre-assembled in a separate area for the Z4, and then supplied to the assembly line as one complete unit, to mention just one example.

Even with the most advanced modern technology, the human element is still vital, with craftsmanship and experience in the assembly process still essential in building cars such as the Z Series. This explains why this phase in the production process involves the highest percentage of manual labour. The assembly specialists work in teams, these accompanying each Z4 in the production process, moving along on transport lines covering several jobs at a time, each team member assuming tasks in line with his or her particular skills and abilities.

The vast array of options in areas such as colour schemes, interior trim, wheels/sizes and engines, to say nothing of the accessory catalogue, means that cars coming off the assembly line are virtually always custom-built to the customer's specification. This is a BMW feature, and quite unlike more mass-production makers such as Ford or General Motors, for example.

continued overleaf

The Z4 Design, Development and Production Processes *continued*

Therefore reliable allocation of the supply of component parts is obviously essential to cope with this enormous complexity. Customer-specific features such as the engine, seats and the cockpit must always arrive at the assembly line at exactly the right moment and in exactly the right sequence in order to meet the appropriate cars coming along. This is why each vehicle is equipped with a transponder, allowing staff in each assembly phase to immediately identify and follow up the car.

The big moment in the final assembly comes when the engine, transmission and suspension join together to form the drivetrain and are bolted onto the body of the car. In order to automate the processes, production otherwise proceeding at a steady, continuous pace is converted at the point into a stop-and-go cycle allowing the workers to fit together the body and the drivetrain with the necessary precision.

Then comes the last step in the production process, which BMW refers to appropriately as the 'finish', with the car being subjected to a function test using sophisticated and highly developed inspection systems and technologies. The axles are measured, the drivetrain, illumination, brakes and on-board electrics checked and verified. Once all relevant checks and tests have been successfully concluded, the new car is prepared for transport and taken to its final destination by truck, train or ship.

Dynamic Stability Control plus Dynamic Traction Control

Another standard Z4 feature is DSC (Dynamic Stability Control). And thanks to the safety reserves offered by the chassis and suspension, the safety system is only activated in critical driving conditions when the limit of normal adhesion is reached – not as an auxiliary function supporting the suspension.

Z4 customers also have the option to enhance DSC to a higher standard by means of BMW's new DTC (Dynamic Traction Control); this provides increased control, especially under slippery conditions. DSC optimizes driving safely in abrupt manoeuvres or in dangerous situations that might suddenly arise in a corner, by applying the brakes as required on individual wheels. A further function of DSC is ASC (Automatic Stability Control) taking back the accelerator pedal and applying the brakes selectively on the drive wheels to avoid any possible loss of traction.

This ASC function has now been enhanced to a higher level in DTC, providing an increase in rear-wheel slip at the touch of a button. Priority is given to traction only at low to medium speeds, then decreasing consistently until reaching medium lateral dynamic forces at around 50mph (80km/h) and/or 0.4g lateral acceleration. The higher wheel-slip level is furthermore adjusted as a function of other factors such as yaw angle and lateral acceleration of the car, all adjusted to current driving conditions. The fundamental safety function of DSC is therefore maintained in full, DTC giving the Z4 the same agility as a car equipped with a conventional limited-slip differential, without restricting the DSC functions when the car is driven to the extreme.

Dynamic Drive Control

DDC (Dynamic Drive control) is another innovation on the Z4. Basically, it provides the more sporting driver with additional power when needed. Operated by a button, DDC is featured as either standard or optional, depending on the market; it calls up the power of the engine even more spontaneously in the sports mode, with the Z4's engine management following a more dynamic throttle-control line. This additional sporting performance is accompanied by the steering becoming even more direct and dynamic in the same process, speed-related power assistance provided by electric power steering (EPS) also following a more sporting and dynamic control map.

In addition, if the car is equipped with a sequential mechanical gearbox (SMG) or automatic transmission, DDC will rev up the gears even higher and shift gears more quickly than usual.

Electric Power Steering
The Z4 is the first BMW to feature electric instead of hydraulic power steering. Electric power steering (EPS) is provided with an electric motor on the steering column and a worm gear for steering assistance. Steering forces are transmitted via the steering layshaft to a mechanical steering mechanism turning the front wheels as required via tiebars. Since this allows the steering to be fine-tuned by means of electronic software, EPS ensures very flexible steering characteristics, optimum harmony of the steering damper effect, and feedback from the road, as well as low steering forces when driving at low speeds and manoeuvring. BMW claims that a further advantage is the 'very good' centring effect, with the steering wheel returning smoothly to its central position after a bend with bumps or vibrations. And by activating the 'sports' mode integrated in DDC ('dynamic drive control'), the Z4 driver is able to reduce the level of power assistance, obtaining an even more direct feeling at the wheel.

Unlike conventional hydraulic steering, EPS does not require any energy when driving straight ahead without the driver turning the steering wheel, thus saving up to 1ltr of fuel every 250 miles (400km) compared with hydraulic steering.

Six-Cylinder Engines
Initially the new Z4 is being built with the choice of two BMW straight-six engines, the 2.5i (2,494cc – 84 × 75mm) and 3.0i (2,979cc – 84 × 89.6mm). The former puts out 192bhp at 6,000rpm against the larger

unit's 231bhp at 5,900rpm, with performance figures of 0–62mph (0–100km/h) in 7sec and 5.9sec respectively, and maximum speeds of 146mph (235km/h) and 155mph (250km/h).

The infinitely variable double VANOS, four-valves-per-cylinder, adaptive knock control and individual coils are all features of the six-cylinder engines carried over from the final Z3 Series (although a 2.5 version was never offered). In their basic configuration, the latest BMW six-cylinder engines on the Z4 are the same, with one significant difference (apart, of course, from the bore and stoke measurements): the intake and exhaust system, as well as all other components of the 3.0-litre engine exposed to intake air, differ in their design in the interest of minimum flow losses and maximum cylinder charge ensured by an optimum resonance effect. In doing so, BMW's engineering team has managed to create a more throaty and provocative sound track. In fact, strangely, I first encountered this more sporting 'fruity' sound track when driving one of the latest E46 325ti Compacts; quite different and much more evocative than that found on previous BMW sixes.

The technical way this has been achieved is by special turbulence ducts on each cylinder, refining the resonance intake system, and speeding up the flow of the fuel/air mixture at lower speeds and engine loads. The result is an improved fuel/air mixture, allowing a retarded ignition angle and helping to further reduce both emissions and fuel consumption. Together with the options provided by infinitely variable double VANOS, this provides far more opportunities to optimize the fuel/air mixture than with a conventional system. The exhaust catalysts, with their high-cell-density metal substrates and thin walls positioned close to the engine, ensure full achievement of the ULEV and EU4 emission standards, meaning that in Germany, for example, both the 2.5i and 3.0i Z4s qualify for a lower rate of road tax (but not in the UK).

Roll-over bars are standard on the Z4, as is the integral boot lip.

Electronic Throttle Butterfly

To allow the Z4 driver to be more precise in stop-and-go traffic and at the same time provide maximum engine power immediately it is required, the six-cylinder power units come with an all-electronic throttle butterfly. The system 'sees' in which gear the car is currently running, and is thus able to activate an individually programmed butterfly control map with the specific features required for each gear. A further advantage of the electronic butterfly is that it keeps transitions from, say, overrun to part-load and vice versa, smooth and harmonious – a feature the driver will also appreciate when using cruise control (standard on the Z4 3.0i model), also integrated in the electronic butterfly.

Five or Six-Speed Gearbox

On the outgoing Z3 Series, even on the M-badged cars, there was only ever a five-speed gearbox, simply because the M Series saloon's six-speeder wouldn't fit. Not so with the Z4,

as the 3.0i comes as standard with a six-speed manual transmission (the 2.5i has a five-speed box). The close-ratio gear increments on the six-speed gearbox, in conjunction with short and crisp lever travel, enable the driver to make the most of the engine's performance. Also available as a cost option on the 2.5-litre car together with SMG, the six-speed gearbox has the further advantage of providing a broader overall gear spread, reducing engine speeds in top gear, which in turn means lower noise levels and improved fuel economy (up to 4 per cent), compared with a five-speed gearbox.

Shift-by-Wire with SMG

As an option, both the 2.5- and 3.0-litre Z4s will be available from spring 2003 with six-speed manual transmission featuring SMG (sequential mechanical gearbox) technology. As a shift-by-wire system, SMG allows the driver to change gears either on the conventional gearchange lever in the centre of the car, or via two paddles on the steering wheel, as used in Formula 1 racing. Above all, SMG is meant to appeal to the most sporting driver, reducing gearshift times to a minimum of just 0.15sec, with what BMW describes as 'absolute precision and consistent shift operation, since the driver is not required to operate a clutch pedal'.

The core function of SMG is changing gear manually with 'unparalleled speed and precision'. The succession of gears is always sequential, with one gear after the other, as on a motorcycle, and not with random, direct selection of a specific gear as with a conventional H-shift gate pattern almost universally found in the four-wheel world. The advantage of the former is that the driver cannot get the gears wrong even when changing gear very quickly, but can nevertheless skip gears whenever appropriate. To shift up, all the driver has to do is either pull back the gear lever or pull one of the two paddles. To change down, he or she performs exactly the reverse operation, either pressing the gear lever forward or pushing the paddles to the front. A further advantage of the paddles is that they allow the driver to change gear without taking his hands off the steering wheel. And the driver is not even required to take his foot off the accelerator pedal when changing gears, the system automatically giving interim fuel in between when changing down.

The Ideal Programme
By pressing the DDC (dynamic drive control) button, the Z4 driver can switch from the more comfortable basic programme to a sporting and dynamic gearchange programme and vice versa. And choosing the sports programme with DSC (dynamic stability control) deactivated, the driver can also use the car's full acceleration. To do so, he has only to press down the accelerator pedal quickly and completely, increasing start-off engine speed to approximately 4,000rpm before the system engages the clutch. This allows even the less experienced driver to achieve maximum acceleration. Normally, the clutch engages at approximately 1,300rpm.

The driver can also use the kick-down function in the manual and drive modes when shifting down, for example when overtaking. A safety programme ensures that the transmission will not change down until engine speeds have been reduced sufficiently without the risk of over-revving. This automatic upshift and downshift gear control avoids critical engine speeds and makes sure that the engine cannot be stalled.

Comfort Shift
BMW calls it 'comfort shift', a drive programme for use in slow, heavy traffic. Besides its sporting side, SMG also has its crawl function. In D (drive) mode, the system changes gear automatically as a function of road speed, the position of the accelerator pedal, as well as increase and decrease in speeds being taken into account. Manoeuvring is achieved by a crawl function activated as soon as the driver, after changing to a forward or reverse gear, takes his or her foot off the brake without accelerating. In this case the clutch will operate with higher slip until the driver presses down the accelerator or brake pedal, in the former case engaging, in the latter disengaging the clutch. A temperature control function protects the clutch from excessive wear.

BMW describes the SMG as being 'grafted' onto the gearbox – the entire electrohydraulic unit being placed on top of the gearbox – like a kind of bell. Communicating with the Motronic engine management, the SMG control unit masterminds engine torque during gearshifts, enabling the driver to keep the accelerator pedal down whilst changing gears.

More Options

Like the majority of BMWs, the Z4's options list is vast. These include not only engines, gearboxes and wheel/tyres but the following:

- Paint finishes, including metallic;
- Cruise control;
- Hi-fi systems;
- Cloth, leatherette or leather upholstery;
- Chrome line trim;
- Cup holders (standard on US cars);
- Power hood (fully automatic operation);
- Aluminium rear carrier;
- Hardtop (from autumn 2003);
- Bi-xenon headlamps;
- Satellite navigation with DVD memory;
- Aerodynamics package.

Index

174